A LIFE OF KINGDOM SERVICE

Douglas W. Crabb

Reflections, Essays, and addresses
of Dr. William B. Coble
Professor of New Testament Studies
1960–1990s
Midwestern Baptist Theological Seminary
Kansas City, Missouri

Compiled by Douglas W. Crabb
Faculty Assistant, 1988–1990
Midwestern Baptist Theological Seminary
Kansas City, Missouri

ISBN 979-8-89243-787-5 (paperback)
ISBN 979-8-89243-788-2 (digital)

Christian Faith Publishing
832 Park Avenue
Meadville, PA 16335
www.christianfaithpublishing.com

Printed in the United States of America

In Loving Memory

Dr. William B. Coble
July 26, 1919–May 31, 1999

CONTENTS

Preface

This material was gathered and gleaned from conversations with Dr. Bill Coble during the years 1988–1989. I served Midwestern Baptist Theological Seminary as a faculty assistant, under an eighteen-month appointment by Dr. Vernon Davis. One of my assignments was to gather articles and materials written by Dr. Coble along with interviews and transcripts of interviews to accumulate what could be gathered before his health failed him completely.

Throughout that year, we met often, and I sought to put the material you have in your hands together.

I asked Dr. Coble how he would want to be remembered. He told me that he wanted to be remembered as a servant of God.

Dr. Bill Coble was a much-loved professor by both conservatives and moderate seminary students. His classes were always full, and students seldom missed his lectures. On one occasion, in a class about 1 Corinthians, he sprung a test on the class, and in some state of panic, the class members attempted to answer by writing the answers to the questions. In part, the test came about because of the often-asked question by students: "Dr. Coble will this be on the final?" On this day, the pop test was his way to preempt such a question.

When it was all said and done, and he had graded the tests, the entire class failed the exam and had to take another test! The lesson was clearly learned. Treat everything as if it is going to be on the final test.

Upon Dr. Coble's death, I delivered a copy of this material to his wife, Mildred, for her and Dr. Coble's children to have. After several years, I found myself in Denton, Texas, accepting the pastorate of Gribble Springs Baptist Church in Sanger, Texas. One of the first questions asked me by one of the members was, since I had attended Midwestern Baptist Theological Seminary, did I know Dr. Bill Coble? To my amazement, I was serving as pastor of a church he had served as pastor during his 1955 years in Denton, Texas, area. He was fondly remembered by some in that church whom he had influenced.

On the following page is a letter Dr. Coble wrote to Dr. Vernon Davis about the work he and I were engaged in.

Dr. Coble certainly modeled humble servanthood to the students at MBTS.

Doug Crabb, compiler, and editor of this material

MIDWESTERN BAPTIST THEOLOGICAL SEMINARY

Telephone 816-453-4600
5001 North Oak Street Trafficway
Kansas City, Missouri 64118

April 25, 1989

Dear Vernon,

    Please let me express another time a sense of deep gratitude for one of your decisions/acts. With it must come an apology for my obvious lack of appreciation for the concept and the effort. Your thoughtfulness in working my stint with Doug is one that I appreciate much more deeply now. Having seen the final form of the work, I see now that it reasonably well expresses the basic shape of my perspective, the base from which I teach. The feeling of doubt that I expressed to you several weeks ago was far more an expression of my overall physical/psychological state than an evaluation of the idea or the effort. I am deeply grateful to you for initiating the collection of these statements. At least they can help my kids see more clearly where I was coming from.

    Your choice of Doug can only be applauded. He is a genuine jewel -- already polished. Without him, this effort would have become a fiasco. His contributions to the total enterprise of higher education will be tremendous, and I count it a special gift to have gotten to work thus with him.

        Just one of many admirers,

        Bill Coble

cc, Doug Crabb

There is no way I could adequately express my admiration for you, particularly for the manner in which you conducted this effort. Be assured of my perpetual best wishes.

    WBC.

I am sorry to have been so slow in getting these answers back to you. So far, 1989 has been difficult.

Biographical Sketch

NAME AND POSITION: William Baalis Coble

Professor of New Testament and Greek, Midwestern Baptist Theological Seminary, Kansas City, Missouri. Since 1960.

BIRTH: July 26, 1919: Poteet, Texas

EDUCATION: BA, Howard Payne College, Brownwood, Texas, 1943

ThM, Southwestern Baptist Theological Seminary, Fort Worth, Texas, 1946

ThD, Southwestern Baptist Theological Seminary, Fort Worth, Texas, 1956

Postdoctoral studies, The University of Chicago, 1967–1968

DENOMINATIONAL EXPERIENCE:

Pastor: Macedonia Baptist Church, Hico, Texas

Whitehouse Baptist Church, Whitehouse, Texas

Sycamore Baptist Church, Decatur, Texas

Splawn Baptist Church, Greenwood, Texas

Gribble Springs Baptist Church, Denton, Texas

Interim pastor of churches in Kansas and Missouri since 1961

Director of the Baptist Student Union and Professor in the Baptist Chair of Bible, Stephen F. Austin State College, Nacogdoches, Texas, 1948–1953

Professor in Baptist Chair of Bible, North Texas State College, Denton, Texas 1953–1960

Professor of New Testament and Greek, Midwestern Baptist Theological Seminary, since 1960

MARRIAGE: September 16, 1940, to Mildred Taylor

Three children: Janice, Shirley, Donald

William Baalis Coble:
A Biographical Sketch

Bill Coble's family has both Irish and German roots. His father, Euel Wesley Coble, was from a family that came from Southern Germany in the eighteenth century. They spelled their name in the German way: Kobel. Their pilgrimage to America came by way of Ireland. Some of his family lineage claimed Ireland as their home until the 1800s when they migrated to the states. They settled on the east coast, and in the process of time, the spelling was changed into the English form: Coble. They were essentially agricultural people. His great-grandfather eventually settled in the San Antonio, Texas, area, and the family remained in that area until recent years. Bill's father had three brothers and one sister.

The Coble family has a long Baptist history. His father, Euel Wesley, became active in Baptist life at a relatively early age. A book of the minutes of the church of which the family were members list his conversion and acceptance into the church when he was twelve years old. He also went to the country schools that were available and spent two years in the nearby town of Pleasanton where he graduated from high school. He then went to college at San Marcos where he met Nina Almeda Cowan. They were married in 1915. They were involved in a combination of farming and teaching school.

Bill's mother, Nina, was from a large family that consisted of seven children: three girls and four boys. Nina was the youngest of the girls, but she had three brothers younger than her. Her education consisted primarily of attending the type of school that was available in rural Texas, in the San Antonio area. She then attended two or three years at what was then called the San Marcos Normal School. This was a term used to describe schools where people were being prepared to teach in public school.

Bill's immediate family was smaller. His sister, Iva Eueline, was born in December of 1916. She was named after Nina's sister and Euel Wesley. She was called Eueline. William Baalis was born on July 26, 1919, at Poteet, Texas. He was named after his two grandfathers: William Smith Coble and Robert Baalis Cowan. Baalis was a Cowan family name derived from Jeremiah 40:14, which meant "Lord of joy." Bill's younger brother, Robert Charles, was born in 1932.

The Coble family moved to the lower Rio Grande Valley when Bill was in the first grade. His father began working there as a book-keeper for the United Irrigation Company, which was one of the founding gents of agricultural life in the lower Rio Grande Valley in Texas. When Bill was five years old, they moved to Austin, Texas. Bill turned six in July and started school in September, attending kinder-garten the fall semester and the first grade in the spring. When they moved from the Rio Grande Valley that summer, Bill had completed one-half of the first grade.

The school structure in the Rio Grande Valley was such that a half-grade system was utilized. At the completion of his first year, his mother was convinced that he could handle second-grade work. They started him in the second grade, but it turned out that he was not ready. They eventually placed him back to the first grade. He had a good teacher who was very helpful and encouraging. He eventually went into the second grade where he did well. Once again, his mother became quite confident that he could excel, and as a result, he wound up in the fourth grade the next year. He continued at an accelerated rate the following year and was placed in the sixth grade. He was able to complete his basic education in the school system and graduated from high school when he was still fifteen years old. Texas had only eleven grades at that time. He was selected to be a valedictorian of his class of ten. The accelerated pace created some difficulties for Bill. He was always two to four years younger than those in his class, beginning especially with the sixth grade. This caused him a great deal of difficulty with his peers.

Bill's family was always involved in Baptist work. Very soon after they moved to the Valley, they joined the First Baptist Church of Mission. His father was active in Sunday school work and served as Sunday school superintendent for several years. Bill was also active in Baptist Young People's Union (BYPU), evening services, etc. His family did not miss very many services. He learned a lot about the Bible in Sunday school. He also learned about the process of publicly expressing himself in the BYPU. Although BYPU provided limited biblical training, it did teach him the fact that speaking before people was nothing to fear. That was a very valuable lesson!

Bill's religious heritage included a strong revivalism. In one revival the evangelist was W. Y. Pond. The revival sessions were held in what was called the church annex. It was just a long frame building that was built directly on the ground. The floor was made of dirt. Benches made from one-by-fours and one-by-sixes nailed together were utilized for seating. On Sunday morning of that meeting, Bill and a young friend were seated together. When the invitation was given, Bill remembers "a definite feeling of conviction that I should accept Christ." He was eleven years old, and his buddy was the same age. They were standing toward the rear of the congregation. A woman that had a very high standing in the church—she was a medical doctor named Dr. Parrish—came back and talked to both. She felt that they had reached the point in time when they should respond and accept Jesus as Lord. She wanted to encourage them to do it if they felt that it was the thing to do. They both went forward that day. It was a very meaningful experience. It was a time in which a real commitment was made. Being a Christian was a matter of significant importance to Bill. The appeal was not made based on the fear of death or the idea of a security that when he died, he would go to heaven. The appeal was made on the basis that Christ is the real Lord of life. To that appeal he responded. He and his friend were baptized at the end of the meeting with quite a few others.

Pat Murphy, a red headed Irishman, was Bill's Sunday school teacher during this time. He was also a very influential person. Whatever he held to, he held to it strongly. He was a very effective teacher for boys their age. He made major contributions to Bill's understanding that the Christian life is a matter of a trusting obedience to Christ as opposed to a simple, external membership in a religious organization called church.

The depression hit Bill's family hard during his last year of high school. His parents were struggling to keep Eueline, his older sister, in college. They also encouraged Bill to go to college despite the hardships. After Bill had finished one year at Texas A&I in Kingsville, pursuing a degree in vocational agriculture, his chemistry teacher convinced him that agriculture was not the area where he ought to be. That type of program was for people who knew a little and could get out and in freely with people and carry on programs. He convinced Bill to begin a career in chemical engineering. Bill initially decided to make this change but never got back to A&I. Since his sister was getting up in years for college students, and the family could not support two in college at once, Bill elected to remain out of school and allow her to continue. She went to Howard Payne where she met her husband and was married.

Bill was out of college for two years. He did not return in the fall of 1937 or 1938. His church, the First Baptist Church of Mission, had a very active group of young people. The pastor, J. W. Hickerson, and his wife were well along in years and had no children. They adopted the young people as their primary interest and maintained a very active program for a small church. Throughout these two years, they had weekly meetings in their home of a group that was called the Volunteer Band. Bill participated and learned much about visitation, witnessing, and Bible study. More importantly, this was where Bill met Mildred Taylor, the young woman who would become his wife.

In the winter of 1938, one of his very close friends in the church, Coleman Turner, said, "Why don't we go to Howard Payne and be preachers?" Bill had already made a similar decision that had all but crystallized. He responded, "That's what I am going to do." He and Coleman made this known to the church. They were soon licensed to preach. In the fall of 1939, he started at Howard Payne College in Brownwood, Texas.

During his first year at Howard Payne, he lived with Coleman. His father had built a kind of house-trailer in which they had done some traveling and which was quite usable as a living accommodation. It was small, but it provided a bed, a dining area, a place to store their clothes, and where they could study. They had to find bathroom facilities elsewhere.

The trailer was parked on a lot owned by Howard Payne College, which was directly across the street from the campus. On that lot was an old dwelling place. Most people today would not believe the ramshackle condition of that house. It was called the air castle because air flowed through it very freely. A sizable group of college students stayed in that house. It had several rooms, and two students would live in each room. The students pooled their food money. Each one had to contribute something like eight dollars a month. One of the residents received his food free for being the cook. They had their meals together. Many times, these meals consisted of nothing more than peanut butter, syrup, and bread. Bill and Coleman shared much of that experience with the larger group, although they did their own cooking in the trailer.

That first year at Howard Payne, Bill was introduced to New Testament Greek. He developed a very amicable relationship with his professor, Dr. W. A. Todd. During the year, he really fell in love with New Testament Greek. He spent a lot of time beyond the required class work in this study. He and Coleman also joined a group of students at Howard Payne called Life Service Band. This group was sent out during weekends to churches in the area. That was his introduction to the churches and the process of witnessing and delivering devotionals. At the end of the year, he and Coleman returned to the Valley.

At the beginning of the second year, Mildred Taylor also came to Howard Payne College. They were married in a most informal setting under a full moon on the bank of Lake Brownwood on September 16, 1940. There was no way anybody could have bought a more beautiful setting. It's not a setting commonly used for weddings. Bill's brother-in-law and sister were there, and he performed the ceremony. The entire wedding cost them five dollars. That was the price of the ring—and that price did not come easily.

They lived in a one room apartment about four blocks from the campus. The apartment cost them $10 a month. Bill's parents were in very difficult financial straits at that time. They were able to do very little to help the newlyweds. Mildreds parents had never had any significant financial assets. Consequently, Bill and Mildred were primarily on their own. Bill found various kinds of jobs. The first job that Bill took paid $0.25 an hour. Another job Bill took was in the area of painting and carpentry. He happened to meet a fellow who did painting and carpentry repair work. This painter was long established and worked regularly. Bill took a job with the painter, which paid $0.37 cents an hour. You must remember that a loaf of bread cost a nickel, and a quart of milk cost five cents.

The Texas Baptist General Convention paid all but $15 of a preacher's tuition as well as his wife's tuition. So the only cash Bill and Mildred had to come up with for a semester was $30. Bill also had to spend a certain number of hours working for the campus each week, doing odd jobs that were needed.

Bill took four years to go through Howard Payne because of the necessity of supporting a wife and earning a livelihood. At the beginning of his fourth year, he took a job as a baggage agent at Bowen bus company. The bus company did a thriving business because, in 1940, the government began the construction of a major inductee camp just outside of Brownwood called Camp Brownwood. There was a tremendous number of soldiers and their families that kept coming in and going out. Gasoline was rationed and if people wanted to go very far, they had to ride the bus. Bill worked as a baggage agent and ticket agent. It didn't pay quite as much per hour as the painting job, but he was able to work more hours.

Bill and Mildred eventually were able to live in a house that the college provided. All they had to pay for was the utilities. There were several houses like this one scattered over the town and as one gained enough seniority one could get into them. It was another of those houses that were simply worn out and people had given it to the school. Students today would think they were being treated indescribably badly if they had to live in a place like that! But it was a house!

Bill graduated from Howard Payne College in 1943 with the highest honors. He and Mildred began making plans to go to Southwestern Seminary. Mildred's physical condition was such that she was not able to attend regularly. She completed two years but never graduated from college. During this last year of college, Bill was asked to preach in several churches. Bill didn't pastor at any time during his college life. During that summer he was called as pastor of a little country church near the town of Hico which is in central Texas. Bill served the small Macedonia Baptist Church near Hico for about a year. During that time, he found that the distance from Fort Worth made continuation impossible. Shortly thereafter, he was called to two half-time churches that were about forty miles north of Fort Worth. Bill continued as their pastor until the completion of his work at Southwestern Seminary.

During the last year of his residency in Fort Worth, he began communicating with the Student Department of the Baptist General Convention of Texas. Eventually, in the spring of 1948, they offered him an opportunity to become the first Bible Chair professor and BSU director at Stephen F. Austin State College in Nacogdoches, Texas. Stephen F. Austin College was one of the systems of state teachers' colleges that had been established in the 1920s and the 1930s. Stephen F. Austin College was the next to the smallest of the group of colleges. There was a large percentage of the enrollment at the school who were Baptists. However, many of them never did reside in Nacogdoches, so a major portion of them never took part in Bill's BSU work other than attending some Bible courses.

Bill had not had previous BSU experience. During college, he was forced to devote so much time to work that there was no opportunity to take part in the Howard Payne BSU. Besides, in a denominational school, the BSU is a totally different issue from what it is in a state school. Bill found that he was starting his BSU ministry from scratch. He received much benefit from a one-day visit from Doyle Baird, who was a well experienced student director serving at the North Texas State College in Denton, Texas. Doyle helped Bill get hold of the basic procedures. He also gave Bill a concept of the overall program.

Bill's primary interest was always teaching rather than the BSU work, although considerably more time was spent with the BSU organization. This work did help him to develop personal relationships with students to a degree that would not have been possible if he had only been teaching. He found a great deal of satisfaction in the Bible classes because the response was always strong. The experience of teaching at that level enabled him to come to a deep appreciation of the type of background that lay people have for biblical studies. This appreciation had a great impact upon his teaching process. He has found that a whole lot of what applied to the needs of students in the college are still the needs of the students in the seminary.

Life in East Texas was most interesting. Bill and Mildred went on to develop some enduring friendships there. Bill had moved there while still lacking two courses of residence work as well as the oral examinations and dissertation for the completion of the degree program. His schedule with the BSU program made such completion difficult. He began looking for some other opportunity and talked with Dr. Howard about this situation. In 1953, after five years at Stephen Austin, Bill was transferred to North Texas State College in Denton as a full-time professor in Baptist Chair of Bible. Responsibility for the BSU program was purely supplemental.

North Texas State College had a considerably larger enrollment. The number of students who were engaged in Bible study was considerably larger than he had experienced at Stephen Austin College. Opportunities to preach and serve as interim pastor existed for about three years before Dr. Howard placed him on the same salary basis and working conditions as the BSU directors. Bill's church life was focused on Denton from that point onward. They stayed at North Texas State College until the end of the school year in 1960.

One Sunday night in early March, Bill was listening to the Walter Cronkite news program when the phone rang. With that call, he received the biggest single surprise of his life! Dr. Joe McClain was the head of the New Testament department at Midwestern Baptist Theological Seminary in Kansas City, Missouri. They had been friends at Southwestern Baptist Theological Seminary. Dr. McClain asked Bill if he would consider moving to Kansas City and joining the New Testament department. Bill had assumed that having a major in Old Testament meant that if he ever taught at the seminary, it would be in the Old Testament department. His experience in the Bible chairs had implanted within him the conviction that he simply did not want to teach the Old Testament as such. The idea of teaching the New Testament had never even occurred to Bill. He had taken nearly as much New Testament studies at Southwestern Seminary as he had taken of Old Testament studies. He had also taken four years of Greek study at Howard Payne before moving to Southwestern. The idea was very appealing.

Bill and Mildred came to Kansas City and visited with Dr. Berquist, who was president at Midwestern at that time. They had lunch with the faculty in which they were guests. Dr. Berquist invited Bill to come, and he and Mildred felt that it was the thing they should do. Bill came to Midwestern for an annual salary of $6,000. They had three children: one nearing high school age and the other two were to enter school that year. This salary was a raise. There were many ample opportunities to fill pulpits and serve interim pastorates, which always was a factor in the necessary maintenance of family. It was hard on the family life.

In the first year of Midwestern's life, the faculty consisted of V. Lavell Seats (professor of Admissions, registrar, and dean of Students); Ralph Elliott (professor of Old Testament); William H. Morton (professor of Biblical Backgrounds and Archaeology); Joseph McClain (professor of New Testament and Greek); and Keith Wills (librarian). Classes were held in the education building of one of the downtown churches (First Calvary Baptist Church in Westport). During that first year, the basic buildings of the campus were constructed. The library, the chapel, and the business office were completed. So at the beginning of the second year, classes were held on campus. Six other men joined the faculty that year: Morris Ashcraft (professor of Theology); Roy Honeycutt (professor of Old Testament); Clifford Engle (professor of Religious Education); Dewey Matthews (professor of Preaching); George Thomason (professor of New Testament);

and Hugh Wamble (professor of Church History). In the beginning of the third year, Bill was added to the faculty along with M. Pierce Matheny Jr. (professor of Old Testament); and John Howell (professor of Christian Ethics).

Midwestern was marked by conflict from the very outset. The political structure in the Missouri Baptist Convention was quite active in securing the seminary for Kansas City. It became quite evident early on that they were anticipating being the central figures in the seminary itself. But when the trustees named Dr. Berquist as president, those plans were thrown into confusion. There were conflicts with certain people in that structure from the very beginning. The pretext for this conflict was conservative theology versus liberal theology, but essentially, the conflict was personal. The large percentage of the people who heard these charges took theological statements at face value. The faculty and administration have had to learn to live with this kind of issue. It made one thing very clear: unity within this structure was not an alternative, it was a life-or-death matter.

Very few people could possibly have done the job of organization and maintaining the relationships, the structure, and the morale, then Dr. Berquist did. He made it very clear that each of the faculty had nothing to prove. They were permanent members of the faculty, period. As a result, they had little to be concerned about so far as inner structure conflict was concerned. Dr. Berquist devoted himself to enabling the faculty to get acquainted with each other, learn how to work together, and to work together to develop the kind of seminary that Midwestern has become.

The faculty also had the responsibility of working out the kind of scenario they wanted. Everyone on the faculty was a graduate of either Southern or Southwestern Seminary, or both. These two traditions were present, and they were quite different traditions. They worked out something that represented a part of each tradition. They maintained amicable relationships throughout the process. There has never been any situation involving any form of open faculty conflict. Midwestern is the only seminary Southern Baptists have in which this is true.

The thing that they had to face, in a personal way as well as a corporate way, was a conflict over the book published by Dr. Ralph Elliott entitled *The Message of Genesis*. The book itself is quite innocuous, but it represented an expression from a Southern Baptist, of a perspective that characterized Old Testament study within the self-proclaimed liberal circles of theology. Dr. Elliott openly espoused the JEDP theory and held to the model place of tradition in the formation of Genesis. This meant that conflict was inevitable. Those who had already established their antipathy to the current organization seized upon the book as a means of giving a theological facade to the program. There were several pastors in Missouri at the time who took up the fight. This had far more influence over the trustees than it did over anybody else. Eventually in 1963, during the trustees' spring meeting (they had only one meeting a year at that time period), Dr. Berquist was pushed into a corner where he recognized that there were no good choices, so far as he was concerned. The only way that things could be retained as they were, which included maintaining Dr. Elliot as a faculty member, was for Dr. Elliott to agree not to issue a second edition that was scheduled to be released. The trustees didn't demand that he apologize for any of his positions. He was asked only to remove the book from the market. Dr. Elliott felt toward that book much the way people feel toward their children. He could not possibly accept this demand. As a result, the trustees voted to dismiss him at that time for insubordination.

Several faculty members had sworn that if Dr. Elliott were dismissed, they would also resign. Only one did. He was Heber Peacock, who had come to the New Testament department in 1962. He was a very close friend of all those that had come from Southern Seminary. When Elliott was dismissed, Peacock submitted his resignation. He departed the faculty at the end of the school year of 1962–1963. None of the other members resigned. Midwestern has lived in the wake of the Elliott controversy ever since.

One privilege that was extended to Dr. Coble in the academic year of 1967–1968 was the opportunity to engage in a sabbatical leave at the University of Chicago. He went as a visitor and auditor. Clifford Ingle, professor of Religious Education, also had leave and was there doing work in his field. Ingle was also quite interested in biblical studies, so they attended some of the same classes together. They were given the privilege of residence at the Baptist house provided by the American Baptist Convention. The only thing they had to pay for was meals. The house was an old millionaire's mansion that had been given to the American Baptist Convention.

The most significant aspect of Bill's work at the University of Chicago was his opportunity to study with Norman Perrin. At that time, Perrin was relatively new at the university. It was through Dr. Perrin that Bill became acquainted with the theory and the mechanics of redaction criticism. Redaction criticism was just beginning its heyday at that time. Although Bill had some familiarity with it prior to this sabbatical, he learned a great deal from Dr. Perrin with regard to the background, principles, procedures, and conclusions reached through this method of study.

The first sentence Bill remembers ever hearing Dr. Perrin say was in a seminar he was conducting on the topic of redaction criticism. He said, "This is a study of redaction criticism. If you do not use redaction criticism, I have no use for you!" With that welcome, he went into the study. He was a very gifted man—of that, there is no question! He was quite willing to try what was new. Although Bill never was sold on his total program, Perrin did open up some things for him in the study of the synoptic gospels that have been totally invaluable. The primary exposure Bill had received to synoptic studies, prior to this, was in a setting in which form criticism was "taboo" and no other critical consideration was given. Bill's perspective on the very nature of the synoptic gospels expanded greatly.

The year that followed the sabbatical (1968–1969) was a very enjoyable year at Midwestern. One of Bill's truly significant shocks, however, came on Memorial Day of 1969. He awoke sometime after midnight with a rather severe pain in his left arm. He finally decided to call his doctor. The doctor instructed him to go to the North Kansas City Hospital. They performed an EKG and put Bill to bed. Although he never experienced any severe pain, he did experience a minor cardiac infarction in the rear part of his heart.

Bill spent the month of June in the North Kansas City Hospital. One of the primary reasons for this long stay had to do with some intravenous liquid he received. The nurses were careless and didn't monitor it carefully. Bill received a far greater dosage than was intended and had his first experience with a genuine "high." He has described this experience as feeling as if he was floating, like a bird, in the clouds. He experienced very pronounced sensations of falling, and yet not falling. This went on for quite some time. After this period of pronounced sensations, he eventually passed out and slept for a great while.

Recovery from the attack was rather slow. He was put on quite a few medications. His activities and exercises were greatly limited. In the month of August, he began to get outside and started walking. His doctor insisted that the best thing for him to do would be to return to teaching in September. He made it through the year, but exactly how is still some mystery. He now reflects and wishes that Midwestern would have had the term system then rather than the semester system. He believes that if Midwestern had had the term system, he would have had a little more time off and would have better recuperated.

He had been serving as interim pastor of the First Baptist Church of Bethel in Kansas City, Kansas, since late December 1968. They were nearing the point of inviting someone to come in view of a call. The man they did invite came with the chairman of the deacons to visit him in the hospital. The church did call this man as pastor, so Dr. Coble's interim was nearly up. That was the last interim pastor he held until late 1970s. He served for a brief time at the First Baptist Church of Platte City, which was the last interim he held.

Midwestern begin utilizing the four-week terms in the middle 1970s. Dr. Milton Ferguson, who succeeded Dr. Berquist, recognized that the seminary needed to do something that would present a new face on Midwestern. The carryover from the Elliott controversy had been exceedingly persistent. Students were simply reluctant to even consider coming to Midwestern. The program was designed to consist of nine four-week terms in which a student would attend each class two hours per day rather than the previous one hour. It was viewed by some members of the faculty as a surefire can't miss procedure. Some of the faculty were exceedingly skeptical from the beginning. Two faculty members were openly belligerent about it. Enough agreed to give it a try and view the condition the school was in that the motion to adopt the program passed.

One of the first impressions of the procedure was that no one can sprint all the time with a four-week limitation of time. The only way anybody could possibly cover this reasonable material for a two-hour course was to sprint all the time. Of course, the students wanted to take as many academic courses as they had previously carried. It became a source of considerable conflict among the faculty. The matter came the nearest to producing a real split among the faculty to anything Midwestern had ever experienced.

It lasted several years, at least seven or eight, before even the most resolute of its defenders concluded that the seminary couldn't go on this way. The structure was changed to the current four eight-week terms. This had most of the advantages of a seminary system without most of the disadvantages. The current faculty has been very pleased with the format.

When the seminary began the program, Dr. Roy Honeycutt was serving as dean. He soon was invited to go to Southern Seminary, to an administrative post, which he accepted. He then became dean and eventually president of Southern Seminary. His loss was a great loss to Midwestern because he was a source of great strength and awareness concerning academic procedures and ideals that Southern Baptists need to practice. Dr. John Howell served as interim dean at Midwestern for a year before becoming dean. He held his post for several years and made a number of valuable contributions.

After Dr. Howell's resignation as dean, Dr. Ferguson recommended Dr. Larry Baker as the new dean. Dr. Baker accepted the position and being a man of almost consummate energy, he began effecting quite a few changes in format and policy. The seminary was able to add several new faculty members. Dr. Baker and Dr. Ferguson worked together in developing programs to attract students to Midwestern. These programs became distinctly productive and helpful in the seminary enrollment. Dr. Baker gave Midwestern dynamic leadership. The overall atmosphere on the campus became charged with good things. The seminary had lost some very significant faculty members in the preceding years. In particular, the loss of Dr. Delos Miles and Dr. Morris Ashcraft, who went to Southeastern Seminary to become dean, were losses from which some feel the seminary never did and never will fully recover. Their departure was followed by the incapacitation of Dr. Thomason and Dr. Morton. The faculty was soon badly depleted. Dr. Baker's leadership enabled Midwestern to replace those who had left.

The seminary was particularly fortunate in the addition of Mr. Pete Butler and his wife Joanne to begin the music program at the seminary. Heretofore, the music program had been conducted purely on a part-time basis by teachers primarily from William Jewell College. Pete Butler's contribution to Midwestern is one that would be very difficult to measure. Dr. Vernon Davis as professor of theology and Dr. Hewlett Gloer in the New Testament department were major additions that strengthened the seminary to be able to meet the situation that arose when Dr. Baker departed.

The experience of becoming a senior professor at the end of 1985 led to one that Dr. Coble had not really been able to foresee. Although Dr. Baker knew for quite some time that Dr. Coble would become a senior professor at the end of that year, he had not been able to secure someone to teach the New Testament survey series. Dr. Coble volunteered to teach two series through the spring term. In March of 1986, Dr. Coble became acutely aware of the fact that something coronary was wrong. His strength was almost totally dissipated. He had begun to feel occasional anginal pains. His doctor scheduled a treadmill test for him on the last day of March. That was a test that he flunked very quickly and decisively. He knew he would flunk it because he had not been able to walk any distance without experiencing anginal pains. The doctor wanted him to go immediately to North Kansas City Hospital for heart catheterization to determine exactly what the condition was. He was forthright. He said that the only real option Bill had would prove to be bypass surgery. The only problem was that the seminary had already scheduled his retirement dinner for the night of April 4. The dinner was on Friday, which was also the end of the first week of classes in the second spring term. Bill wanted to be sure that he would not be able to teach those two classes before making a commitment. He made the classes on Tuesday and was barely able to get through them. On Wednesday, before the second class was over, he knew that there was no way that he could continue the process through the term. That afternoon he called the doctor and asked him to schedule his entry into the hospital for Sunday. Having done this, he told Dr. Baker. He told no one else because of the dinner. If it had become common knowledge, he felt the dinner would have been a "wake" rather than an enjoyable occasion. Dr. Baker told Dr. Coble, just before the dinner started, that he had told Dr. Ferguson about his condition a few minutes prior. The dinner was all that Dr. Coble could have hoped it would be. It was an experience that he treasures greatly.

On the Monday that followed the dinner, they did the catheterization and determined that a quadruple bypass was imperative. Mildred brought the things that he needed to the North Kansas City Hospital, and they went from there to the Trinity Lutheran Hospital. On Tuesday evening, Dr. Coble was hurried through a preoperation process. One of the comical things about that process was the fact of having to take a breathing test. The guy who administered the test was literally shocked because Dr. Coble inhaled well enough to bring the float clear to the top! He had never seen that before. This established the fact that Dr. Cobel had good clear lungs.

The next morning, they woke Dr. Coble rather early. He had slept well because they had given him sedatives. The orderlies wheeled him down the hall and took him into a large room. As soon as they were in this room, several people started busily working on him. Dr. Coble was aware that someone was slipping an intravenous tube into his arm vein. That's just about the last thing he remembered.

The operation was very successful. The next four days were very miserable, however, for Dr. Coble although he never suffered any conscious pain. This is supposedly very extraordinary. Most of those he had talked with who had similar surgeries had experienced very severe pain. The first four days, he was semiconscious. He remembers the irritation of the breathing tube upon his tongue. He visited with others later and discovered that the breathing tube usually remained in place for three or four days. That would have been indescribable misery. He was deeply grateful for a pair of good lungs.

The process of recuperation in the hospital was not greatly traumatic. The only severely painful experience he had while in the hospital occurred when the doctor came to remove the tube that they had inserted in order to keep the heart cavity free of blood. It was injected in his side between his ribs. This tube had really caused him no prior problems. He was aware of its presence because it was physically obvious, but he was able to move freely without any discomfort from it. He had assumed it was a little tube. When the doctor came to remove it, he took hold of the tube and Dr. Coble experienced quite a sensation. It was about ten inches long and about the size of a one-half inch gas pipe. It was about that inflexible as well. When it came out the sensation was noticeable.

The next day, Dr. Coble was able to come home. They started him walking while he was in the hospital. They prescribed progressive assignments for every day until building up to forty minutes of activity daily. He felt very grateful for the whole process.

Dr. Coble's influence as an outstanding teacher was recognized in May of 1987. During the spring commencement, he was awarded the Paul B. and Mary Frances Stevens Award for Excellence in Teaching. Dr. Coble was the first recipient of this award.

Bill and Mildred had three children. Two children were girls, and the third was a boy. That which follows is Bill's own description and remembrances concerning his children.

> We were still in Fort Worth. I was in my last year of residency work. I wasn't finished, but we knew that at the end of that year we were going to leave Fort Worth and go somewhere. Our first daughter was born on July 3, 1947. She shared our last year at Fort Worth. We named her Janice Elaine. When she was just turning one year old, we moved to Nacogdoches, Texas, where I began my BSU/Chair Bible work. On October 1,

1950, our second daughter Shirley was born. She always was a tomboy. She was the very antithesis of Janice, who was exceedingly feminine. Just before we left Nacogdoches to go to Denton, I was serving as interim at the First Baptist Church, Lufkin, Texas. I came back from this Wednesday evening prayer. Shirley, who was not yet three years old, started yelling at Janice. "Janice! Janice! Come on! Daddy! Daddy! Daddy!" Janice, in a very patient way, said, "What's to get so excited about, it's just the same old one." That was a complement that I remember with considerable joy! At about the same time, I was in with the girls as they were getting ready to go to sleep one night. They were in bed, and I was there to have a prayer with them. While I was sitting on the bed, Janice, who had recently turned six, said "You know, Daddy, there are two things that I find really hard. One of them is to believe, and the other is to understand." How do you respond to something like that?

We moved to Denton, Texas, in the summer of 1953. We began a seven-year tenure there as a full time Bible teacher. Our son was born on July 3, 1955, the day Janice turned eight. They have the same birthday, and he has always resented it. It seemed to him that it was her birthday being celebrated, and he was merely tagged on! That's one of the advantages of being older, I guess.

Janice was married in 1968 to a local young man named James E. Turpin. They played the second violin together in the junior high school orchestra during the first year we were here in Kansas City. Then they changed subdivisions of the school district. He went to one school, and she went to another for the rest of junior high.

Both went to North Kansas City High School. They started going together then. James did his college work at Phillips University in Enid, Oklahoma. Janice went to William Jewell for one year and then went for two years to the University of Missouri–Kansas City. They were married on June 8, 1968. Janice then went to Enid and completed her college work while Jim did a year's study for a master's degree. At that time, Jim was serving as a youth worker for the Christian Church. Janice joined the church with him. They moved back to Kansas City after they had completed her work.

Jim became a teacher in the North Kansas City school district. He taught for a couple of years and then was drafted. He was one of the last ones inducted. He was scared to death that he was going to be sent to Korea, but instead, he was attached to a chaplain and assigned to an Air Force Base in Germany. So he went to Germany. Very shortly after he left, Janice discovered that she was pregnant. She completed the fall term in the school where she was teaching and then went overseas.

Joel, my first grandchild, was born in Germany. They stayed in Germany for nearly seven months after his birth. Jim got an early discharge because he wanted to go back to school. They let him come back a little earlier than was planned. Janice had to bring the baby back on commercial transportation. Jim had to stay and come back on military transport. Joel has been very much our pride and joy. The other two children that Jim and Janice have are Jessica and Jeremy.

Our younger daughter, Shirley, was engaged three times, but never married. She was a devoted softball player until she got rather banged up in it as well as too old for it. She received her training at Penn Valley Junior College in Kansas City. She took the motel restaurant management course and specialized in food. Through a long series of experiences involving food service, she was invited to Houston to become a director of food services at the First Baptist Church. She stayed there for almost three years and decided that she had all of that she wanted. Since then, she has been primarily in sales, dealing first in foods and then in office supplies and janitorial supplies. She has done well. She is still in the Houston area.

Our son was born on July 3, 1955, in Denton, Texas. He has always felt somewhat put upon by having two sisters much older than him. Of course, they both adored him, but as young girls will, they also used him however they saw fit. He was a fairly small boy for his age. He is not a large man at all. Mildred's father was a very small man. I doubt that he was five feet, four inches. He also had a small bone frame. Don took after him considerably. Although he has my shoulders, the rest of his body is his granddaddy Taylor's.

He went through the school system here in Kansas City. He had a very limited athletic ability. He had some ability in music that he never wanted to use. He went through a very extensive period of rebellion in which he become involved in drugs and alcohol. He was primarily under the influence of one of the most brilliant students a seminary has ever had. This student had a brilliant mind and was a top-notch musician. But for a while, he took an interest in several boys in this area. He was a sufficiently rebellious person who took great joy in being able to guarantee that at least my son would be a rebel. We went through some very difficult times. The only thing that gave us any kind of solace was that one day he wrote us a note in which he said, "I have always known I was loved." I think, ultimately, that fact became significant. Don met and married a girl who was from a very strong Baptist family in Saint Joseph, Missouri. Don and Patty were married in 1979.

Don started his college studies to be a librarian. In his senior year, he decided that being a librarian might not provide opportunities to make an adequate living. So he set out to try some other things. He never finished college. Their first child was a boy who was born in September 1981. They named him Duncan. They later had a daughter named Jamie in December. They decided to leave Kansas City and go over to Tennessee where her parents had relocated. Through Mr. Garrison, Patty's father, Don became acquainted with a man who was in the higher echelons of personnel with the Tennessee Valley Authority (TVA). This man asked Don if he would be interested in taking a test that the TVA was going to give to some selected aspirants. This test would serve as a basis for composing a new class in hydroelectric production. Don said that he would like to participate. He took the test and scored well.

They moved to the side of the first TVA hydroelectric plant in Florence, Alabama, where the classes were conducted. It was a two-year program. The TBA paid him almost as much to take the program as some people get for teaching. He did very well in the program. He served for over two years in a plant near Greenville, Kentucky, as an electricity dispatcher. He then took the opportunity to apply for a job in Johnson City, Tennessee, where the TVA has a hydroelectric plant and a series of small plants. Although this represented a small cut in pay initially, he determined that it was worth the cut in order to get into the area of work he had been specifically trained to do. They now live in Johnson City.

Covenant: Foundations
of Biblical Truth

The term *covenant* is the real foundation stone of the Old Testament. It is the expression used to describe the relationship between God and his people. The word has its background in practice of ancient conquerors. When they took over new land, they customarily broke it into parts and appointed rulers over the separate parts. The offer was made by the emperor to an "underling" that he could rule a certain area under certain stipulated conditions. The offer was the free choice of the emperor. The one who received the offer could accept it or reject it at his own risk. But he could not change the terms. The terms were set by the one who made the offer. The underling who accepted the rulership knew what his rights powers and benefits were. He also knew the responsibility he had to the one who appointed him.

That is basic to the pictures that the Old Testament provides concerning God's initiative and dealing with people. The fundamental assumption from which the Old Testament is written states, "God initiates, and man responds." The essence of sin, as we are told in Genesis 3, was man's desire to have the basic right to determine the conditions of his relationship with God. After the account of the entry of sin into human life, we are given a picture of a rapid expansion of humanity and an equally rapid degeneration into utter chaos.

First instance of the offering of the covenant in the scripture was the covenant that God made with Noah following the flood in the deliverance of his family. God offered Noah a covenant that was marked by the rainbow. The rainbow stood as a symbol of the covenant that never again would God destroy the earth by water. So there would be no need for more arks. But the story of Noah after Noah's family was chosen to perpetuate the race was a repetition of what had preceded the flood: a rapid degeneration of all life.

Against that background, in Genesis chapter 11, we are introduced to a family of a man named Terah and his sons. Genesis 12 begins with the account of God's initiative in choosing one of those sons, Abram, that's the one with whom he would establish a basic covenant. He would proceed in his purpose for humanity through this man and his offspring. You might say that in Genesis chapter 1–2, we are told how God began with nothing and made everything. In Abram, in a distinct sense, God started over with about as near to nothing as he could. Here was a seventy-five-year-old man who had an old and barren wife. These were the two that were to produce the race of people who would be the agents of God's redeeming purpose of the world as a whole: another miracle of creation.

God gave Abram definitive promises: "I will make of you a great nation… Your name shall be great… I will give you a land in which you and your descendants will reside." He was also given a definitive statement of purpose in the transaction: "Through you shall all the families of the earth be blessed." Like the emperor, Yahweh promised to care for his agent. He made the offer meaningful enough for it to be attractive. He left no doubt concerning what was Abram's responsibility.

The promise that is given in Genesis 12:1–2 is God's assurance of providing well for a person in terms that were commonly understood among Semitic peoples. Yahweh made a severe demand of Abram to separate himself from his people and from his roots and go to a new place. He demanded that Abram take up a new mode of life for which he quite possibly might not have anyone's help. This was a highly demanding call. We might say, parenthetically, that the stirring experience by Abram to move toward the West might be compared to the movement from our East Coast to the West. Abram may have been part of a Great Western movement, but to him, the move had personal significance in relation to his faith in God that was not commonplace among the pioneers.

The details of the covenant always must be understood in the light of the stated purpose of the covenant: to bless all people. The book of Genesis, from that point on, is the story of Abram and his family treated in the light of this covenant purpose. And the Genesis story ends with living descendants of Abram, the offspring of Jacob, in Egypt as guest of honor; prosperous, multiplying, and things going very well.

The book of Exodus begins with the same people, generations later, greatly multiplied but no longer honored guest of Egypt. Because of the change of dynasty, they are enslaved. Their position in the land of Goshen and their being Semitics posed, for native Egyptians, a very serious problem. Many of the invasions of Egypt had submitted origins that approached Egypt up through Goshen. So if some Semitic tribe were to invade, Egypt believed it would be endangered by this submitted group occupying that very strategic position.

The story of the covenant is continued in the story of Moses. The call of Moses in Exodus 3 at the scene of the burning bush, the realization that God had given him the responsibility of achieving the freedom of the enslaved, settling them in the land that had been promised to the forefathers, was a life-long dream for him. But now that he has the assignment, it becomes a great fear. Quite possibly this story's most significant contribution to our understanding of human relationships with God is the answer to Moses's question: "When they ask who sent me… 'What is the name of your God?'… What shall I say?" And the answer was "Say I am who I am." The Hebrew could just as easily be rendered, "I will be who I will be." The point of this reply is that the personhood of God cannot be reduced to finite dimensions, which is man's perpetual desire. "Come down to my level so we can be on equal terms" has always been man's wish. God says, however, "We meet on my terms," and he will not be compromised.

With Moses's acceptance of the nature of this relationship with God and the responsibility of leading the people through the struggle that led to the deliverance from slavery and the return to that very mountain itself, we have the second expression of the covenant relationship. In Exodus 19:3–6, Yahweh announced to Israel the terms of his covenant and said, "You have not seen what I did to the Egyptians and how I bore you on eagle's wings and brought you to myself. Therefore, if you will obey my voice and keep my covenant, you shall be my own unique possession, a Kingdom of priests, a holy nation." The people responded, "All that Yahweh has commanded we will do, and we will be obedient" (Exodus 19:8).

A much fuller account of that acceptance is given to us in Exodus 24 in which the people made formal commitment to keep the covenant by obeying God. This form of commitment was accompanied by a rather lavish sacrificial offering in which the covenant was verified by blood. The people, from that time forward, had some sense of being the chosen people of Yahweh. That sensitivity fluctuated greatly with the generations, but Israel never lost the sense that they were in a covenant relationship with Yahweh their God. The willingness to be obedient fluctuated greatly. They had messengers of God who continually reminded them of the meaning of their commitments. But the one thing that pervades the Old Testament is the abundance of evidence of the light manner with which the people responded to the duties of the covenant committed to them.

The personal nature of covenant is expressed in both the author, the purpose, and the commitment. It is not mechanical, it is not legal, it is personal. The people of God are to share and participate in the fulfillment of God's purpose. The foundation of that covenant relationship was given in what we call the Ten Commandments, found in Exodus 20. The nature of the people's relationship to God is that they will worship Yahweh only. They will never reduce God himself to an image. They will not use the power of God for a purpose contrary to his nature. Those were the vows they took, as well as remembering and honoring his by ceasing to labor every seventh day. The very joy of the covenant was implied in that sabbath day: a time for relaxation, for family fellowship, for rejoicing, for celebration! In neither statement of the Ten Commandments, Exodus 20, or Deuteronomy 5, is formal worship even mentioned. It is a day of rest and celebration to the glory of God. The rest of the commandments were expressions of the standard of life in which each person recognizes the sanctity of his own life and the life of every other person with whom he relates. The very basis of the covenant is personal relationships based on the character and the nature of God.

These commandments bring into clear focus the essentially personal nature of all aspects of God's standards for his people. Naturally, they begin with our relationship with God. The first three are negative in nature. "You shall have no other gods before me." God's people cannot worship any person or thing other than God. "You shall have no graven images." No aspect of God's truth, nature, self-revelation, or purpose can be legitimately expressed in a tangible or visible form shaped by human hands. This prohibition is the background for the prophets' attacks on concerning those seeking to serve God acceptably by doing that which is visible and tangible. The third command "You shall not use the name of the Lord your God in vain" has nothing to do with cursing or swearing. Rather, it forbids calling on the name of God to support, sustain, or legitimize any pattern of conduct that is contrary to his holy nature. We cannot manipulate God for our own egocentric purposes. The fourth commandment is a reminder of the fact that God is gracious, generous, loving, and seeking nothing but good for his people. The command to rest every seventh day was an expression of God's goodness and the fact that he seeks to bring joy into people's lives. In neither Exodus 20 nor Deuteronomy 5 do we find any mention of worship on the seventh day. It was a day for people to relax, relax, and have a good time. There was a time for recognizing that God is the source of all good things and honoring his name by enjoying a release from labor. Thus, the very essence of God is established as One who refuses to be modified or tempered. He refused to be identified with any aspect of impurity or wrongdoing. He focuses on helping people understand his gracious nature.

The commandments dealing with human relationships between each other are likewise anchored in personal and relational concepts. The fifth commandment to honor your father and mother is the very base of social stability. The young supposed that their view of life is naturally as authoritative as that of anyone else. The folly of youth can very quickly be illustrated when it is given a chance to exert itself.

Honoring the parents is recognizing the validity of the wisdom that comes from experience. Such wisdom builds a strong society.

The command "You shall not kill" underscores the sacredness of human life. The word *kill* in this statement poses a problem because the word used meant you shall not murder. Many aspects of the law prescribed capital punishment. Capital punishment was, however, never an individual affair but was always a duty and act of a group when an individual demonstrated himself unfit to participate in society. To allow such a person to continue to live meant people were unwilling to face an unpleasant task to maintain the high standards of life set out in God's directions.

The command "You shall not commit adultery" is a part of the structure that demonstrates the vital importance of the human body and of the marriage relationship. Human sexuality is a part of God's creative design. That design pointed toward the building of a stable society. As many cultures, through the course of history, have illustrated, for people to act as though it is their right to do whatever sexually desirable is catastrophically destructive both to the individual and to society. With the general practice of adultery there can be no stability in family life. There is no sanctity to the home. Thus, adultery is a violation of and a potential destruction of the most sacred personal relationships that exist between human beings. The tenth prohibition, "You shall not covet," shows that the entire list rests on a spiritual base, so none of the other nine can be kept by maintaining an outward form. These essential laws and spiritual principles were the base of all the Torah.

The "ten principles" already discussed are essentially the basis for the ideas that are involved in the instructions provided for the proper and appropriate worship of the Lord. This is also true concerning the relationship of people toward each other and family and in social groups. The focus of all things, both social and religious, is the personal relationship between the Creator-Redeemer God and the persons who constitute his people.

So far as their concept of their relationship with Yahweh was concerned, the Hebrews tended to look upon him as essentially another manifestation of Baal. And they often tended to worship in terms acceptable to Baalism as opposed to the standards set up in the book of Torah, which called for uncompromising loyalty to Yahweh.

Parallel to the emphasis upon the people's refusal to be faithful to their commitments (which had to be renewed with every generation) was the fact that with all of Israel's disobedience, idolatry, misuse of funds, and misuse of people, Yahweh maintained his covenant. He initiated and sustained it because his purpose had not changed—to use these people as his agents to bring life to all mankind.

When the two kingdoms of Israel and Judah were destroyed, the significance of the covenant took on a new shape. When the people were first introduced to Yahweh in a dynamic way, they became convinced that Yahweh truly was "God" in Egypt. There was a demonstration of the defeat of the Egyptian nature gods. They were also convinced that Yahweh was "God" in the wilderness because he provided for them and judged them. The great struggle that Israel had in its history was determining whether Yahweh truly was "God" in Canaan. From their perspective, the land was already inhabited by deities as well as by people. The struggle with Baalism was, therefore, perpetual. But when Judah was destroyed as a nation, the remaining people faced a far greater question. Those who were deported to the area of Babylon had to face the question, is Yahweh "God" in Babylon? It was only through the faithfulness of a relative minority of the people that, beyond any question, those people of Judah became convinced Yahweh was also "God" in Babylon, which is the basis of a truly universal religion growing out of that ancient and very primitive concept of covenant.

When the people who wished to run the risk return from Babylon to Judea, the great question remained: "Is Yahweh truly 'God' in this land?" They committed themselves without qualification to the fact that he still was "God." But they became quite a different people from their forefathers because they reduced service to Yahweh to a combination of practice rituals and legal rules to be obeyed. This combination of legalism and ritualism was the dominating force through much of the period between the return (roughly around 445 BC) until the time that Jesus was born.

Jesus entered the life of a people whose sense of covenant relationship was brought to focus on ritual forms and rules of conduct. The struggle that Jesus had was a struggle with ritualistic, legalistic, religious people who were thoroughly convinced that they and they alone were living out the implications of the covenant that Yahweh had given their forefathers in the wilderness. Jesus's purpose was to show those people that the relationship God had initiated with his people had been, from the beginning, personal in nature. It could not be reduced to ritualism. It could not be reduced to legalism. Yahweh, the God of Israel, is a living person who purposes to relate to his people at the personal level, which means that the totality of life is to be lived with a sense of his indwelling presence leading to a life of voluntary service to the achievement of his intended purposes. This understanding enables the world to see and understand the true nature of the God of Israel. This understanding also invites the world to be participants in service to him.

The sense of the dramatic change in emphasis is brought to focus on both Matthew and Luke, in which we are given the picture of Jesus with his disciples at Jesus's last observance of the feast of Passover. When the festival observance had concluded, we were told of his taking bread and the cup and instituting a new covenant when he said, "This is the blood of a new covenant." He let the disciples know that his own death was, in a sense, a reenactment of Exodus chapter 24 in which not the blood of animals but the blood of a person was shed in order that people might understand the unlimited, unqualified love that God has for people.

Covenant: Related Issues

One of the problems we have is the way the term *testament*, which is a derivative of the Latin word for *covenant*, has been substituted for the word *covenant*. Our people are not familiar with the covenant concept. They have little understanding of the truth to which Abraham was introduced in which Yahweh regarded Israel as a living person and relates to his people the level of personhood. God's purpose is to shape them and their lives in accord with his own nature that they might become "sharers" of his personhood and be exemplars before the world of the living, spiritual relationship with this supreme person.

Marriage is the most used symbol of the "covenant" in both the Old and New Testaments. The emphasis upon the historical background of the Hebrew term *berith*, which is translated "covenant," was simply to show that it was something offered freely by one who is the true authority. Its primary requisite is personal relationship, submission to one who has the right to control. That is the common point that gives the term *covenant* its meaning. Until the recipient of a covenant is aware of the fact that he has been graciously blessed by the offer of a very meaningful personal relationship to his supreme being, he cannot appreciate the message of the gospel. Although marriage is the most effective symbol, the one thing that serves somewhat as a barrier to its effectiveness as a symbol in our time is the recognition that marriage is now an agreement between equals, which was not the case in Israel in biblical times. Every analogy to the covenant that we can use, if pressed to its ultimate application, breaks down.

Obedience, in the sense of covenant relationship, is what would be looked upon as the normal response to an opportunity extended to a lesser from a greater. The only thing that could cause the concept of obedience to be a problem for this lesser one is pride. This is true because in the covenant that is offered one becomes so much more than he could ever be in isolation. The opportunity of a living relationship with him who is creator and controller of all things is a privilege that none of us has any right to demand. It is freely offered. The essence of acceptance of the offer is the recognition of the true status of the participants in acting accordingly. In one sense the very nature of the covenant means "God is boss." We have the opportunity to live under the most benevolent and gracious of "bosses" who act only out of love for us and the desire for us to experience that for which we were created. The alternatives we have are anything but gracious and benevolent.

It could be said that the sovereignty of God is basic to the covenant concept. The great problem of the legalist is the determination to be in control. The very essence of the covenant is humble submission to one who is rightful ruler. Legalism is so attractive to many people because it leaves them with a sense of being in control. The sense of the underling being in control is the antithesis of acceptance of the covenant. The essence of accepting the covenant is the willingness to enter into a living, personal relationship with God that has characterized primarily, in our lives, by voluntary submission to what we know of his will.

The word translated "sin" can be understood in its biblical sense only if we remember that essentially it is a term that has its meaning in the light of God's covenant with his people. "Sin," in its essence, is personal rebellion against the legitimate overlord. The whole matter of our relationship with God is one of human beings' willingness or unwillingness to be let God be God. Do we seek to exercise, on our own, the prerogatives that only rightly belong to God? To fully understand "sin," we must go back to the essential nature of the covenant as a relationship established by the degree of a superior. The primary requirement of the one who receives the benefits of the covenant is the response of obedient trust. The direction of one's own life to the fulfillment of the purposes of God, and the attainment of his goals to the degree that he/she is willing for life to be an instrument for the achieving of his purpose, determines whether he truly is obedient to God.

When we seek a kind of relationship with God in which we have access to personal favors that can be achieved and used through the attainment of our own ideas apart from his will, we are truly living the life of rebels. So the matter of the identity of any particular act becomes totally secondary. There are many points at which the most openly licentious and immoral sexual conduct becomes totally insignificant in comparison to a manipulative attitude by which one seeks to give the impression of being totally devoted to God when he is seeking only to use an association with God as a means of achieving his own particular purposes. This is true, however noble those surprises may be. Sin is essentially a rebellion against a person who has the legitimate authority and right to direct and control life. This is the reason why we must understand sin in light of the covenant.

The term *egocentricity*, or self- centeredness, comes as near bringing the meaning of sin into sharp focus as does anyone expression. To go back to the scene of Genesis 3, what we are told is that the two human beings simply took what God had made available to them and determined to use it in accord with their own purposes for their own benefit in open violation of God's direct instructions concerning how to use the things he had provided. The reason that lay behind that act was the temptation presented by the tempter, "If you do as I suggest you will be just like God you. You will have total control of your life."

The great human desire has always been to be able to control life rather than be controlled. The tragedy is that we were not equipped with the necessary gifts, capacities, and perspectives to be in control. We are so made that we can give true expression to ourselves only in obedience to one who is far greater than we. So when we determine to try to use God for the attainment of our own ends we have the nature, the meaning, and the purpose of life completely inverted. Rather than attaining the highest we are capable of attaining, we destroy ourselves by rendering impossible the attainment of that which we were made to attain.

Sin is, in a sense, though both self-denial and self-rejection in the name of the desire to exalt and approve upon our perceived selfhood. Those who are made to be servants can ill afford the ambition to be Lord's. The two great commandments are to love God completely and to love our neighbor as ourselves. Egocentricity means that we are trying to use God to achieve our purposes.

Much more directly, we seek to use other people to achieve our purposes. Making others the instruments, of our ambition is an open expression of our complete willingness to destroy another individual's personality. This is the true disastrous significance of egocentricity, of sin. Sin is also, by nature, a social event. It is not something that takes place in one person's isolation. By its very nature, sin involves a plurality of people and is destructive to all. Nobody profits.

The term *law* is another of those words that is exceedingly difficult to fit into modern expressions of thought. To us, "law" means a "rigid rule" or "a statement of acceptance or unacceptable conduct," any violation of which calls for some stated punishment. There are, however, many slight variations of the concept, such as "the law of averages," or "the law of cause and effect." But when we talk about human conduct in light of the law, the word does not connote some kind of rigid rule, violation of which demands some form of punishment. When people today hear of law and religion, they understand it in terms of rules. This further means that if salvation is by faith, then law no longer has any bearing on their relationship with God. Consequently, there are no particular guides to conduct.

This understanding causes some very difficult problems. When Paul used the word *nomos*, he was using a Greek term that is very closely related to our concept of law. In his mind, however, the issue was "Torah." "Torah," a Hebrew word, did not mean a fixed rule for which rigidly assigned punishment was applied. Rather, the "Torah" constituted a guideline, an ideal, and a high statement of purpose.

As Paul viewed the Torah, he realized that in many ways it had been a source of blessing in his life. The Torah had provided an indicator of the nature of God and the nature of God's purpose for his people, as well as God's standards for his people's conduct. But as Paul saw both his fellow Pharisees and the Judaizers within the Christian movement dealing with "law," he became well aware of the way that they had come to deal with the law as we think of "law." So as Paul dealt with the relationship between law and grace, he was aware that such an understanding of "law" had no legitimate place in the gospel of good news about God's grace. This is the reason why Paul chose Abraham as his model for a Christian understanding of the gospel. Abraham responded with a purely personal faith, obeying God's command to leave the land where he was secure and prosperous, going to the land where God would bless him, his descendants, and the whole world. Such an obedient response of trust constituted, for Paul, the essence of Old Testament teaching which was epitomized in the term *law*.

One of my great fears and a source of fear is the seemingly obvious evidence that the people of our time have no more concept of the significance of God's covenant relationship than did the people who returned from Babylon. This is the reason why our churches are marred by legalists and ritualists who obviously manifest no sense of a living relationship with God whose primary trait is self-giving love. The persistence of that self-giving love is as manifest today as it was in any point in Israel's history. So we have every reason to try to help people understand the meaning of covenant.

Covenant Distortions

The purpose of this whole line of thought is anchored in the creation story where it is recorded that God created humanity in his own image and his own likeness. This means that we have the capacity for full personhood in a manner that is comparable to God's own nature. By this we are greatly blessed. Because of this we are also faced with many problems. The story of the temptation and fall is an account that shows the essential egocentricity with which human life manifests itself. Such egocentricity includes the attitude that self should be in control and what self-experiences and desires represents what is legitimate in God. The story of Genesis portrays the whole concept of the covenant people as having its beginning in the call of Abraham in Genesis 12. In this story, the promises of the covenant and the purpose of the covenant are clearly brought into focus. God's aim is that through Abraham and the covenant all peoples of the Earth will be blessed. The rest of the book of Genesis is a story of Abraham and his family living essentially in the land of Canaan under the awareness of this kind of covenant relationship with God. But before the book concluded all the descendants of Abraham, Isaac, and Jacob were in Egypt. There, the book of Genesis leaves them in a state of high privilege and honor.

The book of Exodus opens with them still in Egypt. They are greatly extended in numbers but tragically debased to the state of slavery. The expression of the covenant with these descendants of Abraham, Isaac, and Jacob, which was manifested in the great redemptive act of the Old Testament, the deliverance from Egypt. In Exodus 19:1–6, we have the statement of a new covenant relationship given to the people. The purpose of that covenant was that this whole people become the instruments of God, serving as his priest among the earth's people.

The whole covenant is primarily redemptive in nature. God purposes to bring all mankind to the realization of the fulfillment that is implied in our being made in his image. This hope can be attained only as those who know God personally serve faithfully as his interpreters within the nations.

The statement of the cabinet very clearly involved obeying his voice by keeping his covenant and living by it. The standards of that covenant relationship were set out in exceedingly brief form in Exodus 20, which we call the Ten Commandments. These standards are the basis of the covenant relationship between God and his people. At least they are the base of the manifestation of the fact that these people are faithful to God and willing participants in his purpose for the nations.

Materialism

The first two commands were explicit: no other gods, no images. Almost before the ink had dried on the parchment we find, in Exodus 32, that the people, because of some dissatisfaction with schedule, immediately produced for themselves an image to worship and desired to go back to Egypt as though nothing of any real significance had happened in their covenant commitment. This experience stands as a constant object lesson to the fact that words alone establish no dependable reality. The tendency among the people of Israel to turn to other gods when the God of the covenant seemed *not* to be producing according to reasonable expectations is the very heart of their problems throughout history.

As soon as Israel settled in the promised land they encountered the problems of the very basic idolatry of human life, Baalism. The Baals were the personification of materialism. When Israel settled in the land, they were informed that unless they offered the appropriate sacrifices to the Baal of the immediate area, they had no hope of any success as farmers or as cattlemen. Thus, the first part of the history of Israel is the struggle between faithfulness to the covenant of a personal God and the appeals of pure materialism. The promise of the Baal's seemed so easy and seemed so often to have been fulfilled. This promise indicated that if one offered the right sacrifices and did the proper rituals to the proper deity, the deity would see to it that prosperity was dependable and constant. Yahweh never did make such a promise on such easy terms.

Materialism has been the great abiding idolatry through the ages. Idolatry is nothing more than our attempt to share God in our own image and to force God to act in ways that conform to our own desires, standards, and goals. This initial form of idolatry has plagued the people of God from the very beginning.

The materialism that is involved in today's expression of Christianity in this country lies blatantly on the surface for all to see. The promises of prosperity, security, good health, and long life if people conform to whatever demands a messenger may present in church, over the radio, or on television (the medium does not matter) reflect such idolatry. The persistence of the idea that faithfulness to God brings personal, and particularly, material prosperity is one of the persistent thoughts people have had to weigh throughout the ages.

The problems of Baalism make up a large portion of the history of the people of Israel from Joshua through conquest. One thing that we find in the prophetic books, particularly in Jeremiah, is that the people of Israel continued to live by the worst possible form of distortion as long as they were in the land. The great sin of Israel was not open, blatant Baalism. The great sin Israel was their official, public declaration of the rejection of Baalism and their total devotion to Yahweh as their God. Having made the public statement, however, for the most part they worshipped Yahweh as though he were Baal, attributing to Yahweh traits totally rejected in the covenant statements.

Ritualism

A second element, or step, in the idolatry of the covenant people was also directly connected with the avowed loyalty to Yahweh. This step has to do with the localization of God and is evident in the story of David, which is one of the central stories of all scripture. In 2 Samuel, we're told of David's military successes, his having established an extensive kingdom in which peace prevailed. In 2 Samuel 7, David came up with what he thought was the most appropriate idea. He called in Nathan, his religious adviser, and pointed out that he, as king, was living in a house of cedar while the ark of the covenant, which was the emblem of Yahweh's presence among his people, was still being housed in a tent. It was movable. It had no permanent abode. It could go wherever people needed it to be.

David suggested that it was only appropriate that the ark of the covenant should have a house fully as befitting the royalty of Yahweh as David's house befit him. The immediate reaction of the preacher was "Sure, let's have a new church. Go ahead and build it." David did not realize that in the process of building the temple, you begin the process of localizing God, which includes the process of serving God in one place, one established standard of procedures, or rituals. David did not get to build the house, but he was promised that his son, who would succeed him to the throne, should build it. When Solomon came to the throne, he took the plans which David already had made, and the temple was built in all its grandeur.

This event gave rise to the second element of efforts to shape God in their own image. As far as I can see, the only appropriate term for this element is *ritualism*. Having God localized in a highly developed system of religious forms made matters rather simple for people who wanted to fulfill their religious duties to God without having to get too involved with their neighbors.

A large portion of the writings of the prophets focuses on this issue: the people's reduced relationship to God and their loyalty to their purpose under the will of God as being the offering of ritual sacrifices. This involved the performing of a great variety of rituals. Thus, they forgot that the covenant was based upon standards of personal relationship with the living God as well as the manifestation of this relationship through his standards of relating to other persons. Rituals became the substitute for living, personal relationships with both God and their fellow man.

Isaiah gives one of the most powerful expressions of the tragedy and of the evil that is involved in this process. In the first chapter of Isaiah, he said, beginning at verse 2:

> Hear, O heavens, and give ear, O earth;
> for the LORD has spoken:
> "Sons have I reared and brought up,
> but they have rebelled against me.
> The ox knows its owner,
> and the ass its master's crib;
> but Israel does not know,
> My people do not understand."
>
> Ah, sinful nation,
> a people laden with iniquity,
> offspring of evildoers,
> sons who deal corruptly!
> They have forsaken the LORD,
> they have despised the Holy One of Israel,
> They are utterly estranged.

Isaiah voices this description of the tragedies that had brought upon them, saying in verse 9:

> If the Lord opposed had not left us a few survivors,
> we should have been like Sodom and become like
>   Gomorrah.
> Hear the word of the Lord, you rulers of Sodom!
> Give air to the teaching of our God,
> you people of Gomorrah!
> "What to me is the multitude of your sacrifices?"
> says the LORD;
> I have had enough of burnt offerings of rams,
> and the fat of fed beasts;
> I do not delight in the blood of bulls, are of lambs,
> or of he-goats.

When you come to appear before me, who requires
        of you
this trampling of my courts?
Bring no more vain offerings;
Incense is an abomination to me.
New moon and Sabbath and the calling of assem-
        blies—
I cannot endure iniquity and solemn assembly.
Your new moons and your appointed feasts
my soul hates;
they have become a burden to me,
I am weary of bearing them.
When you spread forth your hands,
I will hide my eyes from you;
even though you make many prayers, I will not
        listen;
Wash yourselves; make yourselves clean;
remove the evil of your doings
from before my eyes;
cease to do evil, learn to do good;
seek justice, correct oppression;
defend the fatherless, plead for the widow.

Isaiah brought to focus the fact that ritual practices can easily become the essence of people's faith in God. By performing the rituals, they hope to be fully accepted by him and recipients of all the blessings he has promised to faithful people.

A major portion of the books of the prophets is devoted to a similar kind of reproach. Nobody can despise people and serve God acceptably. This is the very heart of the book of Amos. In his condemnation of the practices of the northern kingdom, one of the most bitter words of satire of all the biblical writings are in Amos 4:4, where Amos refers to two prominent northern kingdom sites of worship: "Come to Bethel and transgress, to Gilgal and multiply transgressions."

The people's very practice of going through the prescribed rituals when they refused to treat their neighbors in the manner that the covenant demanded becomes an open insult to God.

Probably the best known and certainly one of the most beautifully stated expressions of this fact is in Micah 6:6–8:

> "With what shall I come before the LORD,
> and bow myself before God on high?
> Shall I come before him with burnt offerings,
> with calves a year old?
> Will the LORD be pleased with thousands of rams,
> with ten thousand rivers of oil?
> Shall I give my first-born for my
> transgression,
> The fruit of my body for the sin of my soul?"
> He has showed you, O man, what is good;
> and what does the LORD require of you
> but to do justice, and to love kindness,
> and to walk humbly with your God?

Ritual can be very expensive. One can spend a lot of money on it. But ritual that does not express the gratitude of an individual whose life is lived out of obedience to God's standard of caring for people becomes pure and unmodified idolatry. One would be as well-off worshiping Baal.

The ritualism that exists in our time has a tremendous variety of expressions. Most of the professed Christians of our time demonstrate, in a multitude of ways, that their understanding of what God wants of them is somehow wrapped up in going to church. But Jesus made clear that the worship that we often honor becomes for us a source of misunderstanding. Worshipping God our father becomes a source of inspiration, guidance, and strength to give ourselves in service to those who cannot meet their own needs. To be indifferent to the needs that face us and other persons while we go through the motions of our expression of the Christian faith becomes the modern counterpart of "trampling the courts of the temple" just to impress God with one's presence.

Ritualism went with the people of Judah when they were carried into captivity in Babylon. In Babylon, they had to settle one of the major issues of all theological truth: "Is the Lord God only in ancient Canaan?" They discovered that he is not only in ancient Canaan. They learned that the Lord was also God in Babylon. The basis of a truly universal faith was laid in that captivity experience. When a small portion of those people and their descendants determined to return to the fatherland and rebuild the temple and reestablish the express purpose of God for his people to be his agents of redemption, they also brought their ritualism back with them. We find in the prophets, particularly in Malachi, the fact that when they had rebuilt their temple, their worship still had no higher level than that which Isaiah described.

Legalism

When the people returned from Babylon, they also faced another problem. This was the problem with the place of prophecy in the life of Israel. There was a relatively brief period in which the words of the prophets were recognized. We find this period reflected particularly in the books of Haggai, Zachariah, and Malachi. Prophecy overall, however, lost its standing with people because too many pretended prophets tried to outdo each other promising the people glorious blessings if they remain faithful to the Lord under their very difficult circumstances. When the blessings never came, the people quit listening to the prophets.

This return also reflects the beginnings of a new approach to the faith that had been handed down from Abraham, Isaac, and Jacob. This new approach was centered and focused on the law. As the people studied the standards that were set out in the books of the law, particularly in Genesis through Deuteronomy, they began to give particular attention to the details of ritual responsibilities. As they focused on these formal duties, while maintaining their ritualism, we have the beginnings of a third-grade form of idolatry among God's people. That third form of shaping God in our image we can best call legalism—living by fixed religious rules. Such careful devotion to the requirements set out in the books of the law and trying to apply the standards of the ideas embodied in those teachings caused the people we call Jews (the descendants of people of Judah who returned and resettled the land) to have to deal with three essential questions:

- Who are the true people of God?
- How shall they be identified?
- How shall they relate to the rest of the world?

When the Jews returned from captivity, they all had their pedigrees. They were direct descendants of the people who had been taken away in captivity. Upon their return, they immediately encountered the problem of the Samaritans. The Samaritans were the descendants of the intermarriage between the lowest-class Israelites (which the Assyrians had allowed to remain in their own land when they shipped the great body of leadership out in 722 BC) and Gentiles. Gentiles were present because the Assyrians brought in other people whom they had conquered and settled these people among this residue of the lowest-class Israelites who had already been infected with idolatry since the days of Jeroboam's golden calves. The Israelites intermarried with the Gentiles. The Gentile idolatries mingled with the Israelite idolatries introduced a mixed religion as well as mixed blood (see 1 Kings 12:25–33 for example).

The whole picture led Jews to determine that the only way they could maintain the purity of the faith was to maintain the purity of their identity. They determined that a Jew had to be a lineal descendant of Abraham, Isaac, and Jacob without any mixture along the way. Thus, you have the establishment of a long history of open conflict between Jews and Samaritans. We find the foundation of this conflict in 2 King 17. So when the Jews dealt with the question, "Who are the true people of God?" their answer was "The lineal descendants of Abraham, Isaac, and Jacob." Yet they had a convenient way of circumventing this strict code. Any Gentile who was not a descendant of Abraham, Isaac, and Jacob was allowed the privilege of becoming a proselyte. A proselyte was anyone willing to accept conversion to Jewish religious faith and take up life under the law. After the proselyte was circumcised and baptized, he was treated as one living fully and completely under the Law. His sons were called direct descendants of Abraham, Isaac, and Jacob. But this reflects the conviction that obedience to the Law gave people their true identity. This was the approach utilized in the handling of this matter of birth. Thus, the Jews responded to the second question: "How do the people of God identify themselves?" by answering: "They keep the Law."

The third question was "How did the people of God relate to the other peoples of the world?" Their answer was quite practical: "Just as little as possible, and never on their terms." Through this process of exclusivism, the Jews added obedience to law to the practice of ritual, and they set the tone of the expression of the life of the covenant people who Jesus encountered when he came with a message that rejected both legalism and ritualism as well as Baalism. Jesus's rejection of the currently accepted Jewish standards was the basis of the conflict between him and the Jews which ultimately led to his death.

Jesus's followers, the converts to what we know as the Christian faith, lived for several generations under the dynamisms of his message and indwelling presence of the Spirit. They embodied the basic concept of the covenant, the uniqueness of God, the spirituality of God, and the manifestation of oneness with God, through caring for one another. This kind of life pattern drew the spiritually starved people of paganism to the Christian faith as an open melon draws flies in the marketplace!

Institutionalism

The growth of the early church was both free and unimaginably fast. But as succeeding generations became Christians the group became infected with the same forces that have worked within the life of Israel. When the basic concepts were handed on as family traditions, rather than being each generation's vital experience, the concepts became progressively less dynamic and less life-shaping. The act of Constantine in making the Christian religion the official religion of Rome became a powerful force in stripping the faith of the vitality that had made it such an attraction to those in need.

As a result of numerous forces working together, we have the development of the fourth open manifestation of shaping God in men's image within the covenant people. This fourth manifestation is institutionalism. The church ceased to be a fellowship in which people shared each other's burdens and sought to work together to meet the needs of the world around them. It became an institution that was responsible for maintaining set traditions and set patterns of practice. In institutionalism, the organization is considered the living power. It has the authority to control all of life. It has the power to enforce its will. The individual ceases to be a measure of anything within the institution. The individual is essentially a "cog" within the machine's operations. The individual is not invested with responsibility since with responsibility comes authority, and authority rests within the institution. Institutionalism caused the Roman Catholic Church and other Catholic groups to become authoritarian religionists. Institutionalism introduced Christian persecution of nonconformists. Institutionalism laid the foundation for later conflicts and open warfare among those who disagreed regarding the details of the Christian faith. Institutionalism carried with it all the problems introduced by Baalism, ritualism, and legalism, plus the burdened weight of official power.

Institutionalism controlled most of the basic expressions of the Christian faith for fully one thousand years. Its continuing manifestations have been open and clearly visible. Many of the marks of pure institutionalism are heavily ingrained in the lives of great varieties of expressions of the Christian faith today, as people still do battle over what constitutes the true church, how the true church manifests itself, and what is the place of the individual within the true church.

Institutionalism came into being simply as the manifestation of this aspect of human life that devotes itself to recognized organizations and commitments of oneself to the effective workings of those organizations. It has a multitude of expressions in the problems of Baptist life. One of our great illusions or delusions is the thought that our sense of the "independent church" means that we are able to live above the problems of institutionalism.

The period commonly called the Dark Ages, roughly from the fall of Rome to the beginning of the renaissance about AD 500 to AD 1400, represented the very highest expression of the supreme religious institution in Europe, the Roman Catholic Church. It used every kind of power to force people to conform to the express will of the institution. The will and voice of the church was the will and voice of God. The period shows the truth of the statement that W. T. Conner made frequently, "Whenever men think only they embody the will of God, they invariably act like demons." Institutionalism combined the worst elements of human idolatry.

Theologism

In the Renaissance (roughly from the latter part of the fourteenth century through the early part of the seventeenth century) people began to think again in manners that benefit human personhood. This beginning marked the start of the decline of the power of the dominating institution. Changes of attitude toward church authority stem from convictions that the religious institution can rightly represent God only to the degree that its teachings and practices rightly represent God's character, purposes, and methods. Many groups begin insisting that they or some men whom they followed had discovered that God's character, purposes, and methods differ from those practiced and taught by the Church of Rome. Some demanded that the Roman church modify its teachings and practices so those with the new views could remain within the church. Others demanded their freedom from the Church of Rome and prepared to fight to defend themselves from Rome's claim of authority to control and to punish the dissenters. Some of the groups become free of Rome. Then they began fighting each other because they could not agree on how they had to disagree with Rome.

From the beginnings of the idolatry of institutionalism, the life of the primary "Christian" movement was controlled by leadership who enacted this view of their duty: When you refuse to conform to what we tell you to think and practice, in the name of God, we do what we must to enforce your conformity to our instructions, even if it seems that we hate you.

Under the Roman church, the issue most often was the practice of rituals. As groups began breaking away from Rome, the central issues focused most often on concepts: the reasoning that lay behind the form of the church itself and its practices. So the battlefield moved from the churches to man that all people maintain the institutional churches unity of structure and practice to the issue of conforming of concepts to statements of gospel truth. Growing out of this shift came many life and death struggles: group against group, then splinter groups against splinter groups. This long series of developments led to some of Europe's most vicious and bloody wars, which were fought over details of organizational alignment in theology.

The primary reason this whole process merits the designation "idolatry" is found in the long-standing attitude and expression, "In the name of God, I must hate the terrible error you espouse to the point of seeking to destroy you along with it." This kind of attitude absorbs most of the energy any group has to expand on achieving God's purposes in the world. It is in fact a continuation of various phrases of its predecessors. So the viewpoint openly tells others, "If you are to be acceptable to God, you must understand God's truth as I (we) understand it, teach it as I (we) teach it, and practice it as I (we) practice it." This view is only a duplicate form of the old Roman church dogma: *The word of the church is the word of God.*

Continuing generations have continually multiplied the splintering of self-professed people of the covenant since more and more groups claim openly, "We, and only we, are truly God's people." Thus, those who claim to be God's covenant people become more and more shattered and are progressively making less and less impact on the world. The world, for the most part, now laughs at all who make that claim. The world sees it, in most of us, so little of the kind of love Jesus described in Matthew 25:31–40. That love serves the needy just because they are in need.

Theological idolatry that insists that God conform to, affirm, and bless only those who adhere to my system, continually shatters any semblance of unity among those seeking to embody God's covenant purpose. Is there any hope that God will ultimately achieve the goal that he expressed to Abraham in Genesis 12:3? The only hope I see lies in our capacity to recognize that we all are natural born idolators, tempted constantly to share God in our own image. Then we can remember that only God's gracious love and power can transform us, giving us capacity to embody the ideals of His covenant: genuine personal loyalty to God as both the source and the key to life and giving self to do what we can do to meet whatever needs we face in each life with whom we deal. If we are, thus, occupied, we will have little time or energy to devote to self-praise or in the condemnation of those who are simply being true to the uniqueness that God committed to each person.

The Bible: Its Beginnings and Development

By William B. Coble

The Southern Baptist Convention, in 1963, adopted this statement about the Bible:

"The Holy Bible was written by men divinely inspired and is the record of God's revelation of Himself to man. It is a perfect treasure of divine instruction. It has God for its author, salvation for its end, and truth, without any mixture of error, for its matter. It reveals the principles by which God judges us; and therefore is, and will remain to the end of the world, the true center of Christian union, and the supreme standard by which all human conduct, creeds, and religious opinions should be tried. The criterion by which the Bible is to be interpreted is Jesus Christ." (*The Baptist Faith and Message*, 7)

People have given this statement many interpretations. I would summarize the gist of it thus.

The Word of God

This phrase probably is Baptists' most used description of the Bible. The term implies vital elements of our faith, including at least these points: (1) God is real, living, and active. The Bible makes no effort to prove this truth, but the assumption is the base of all that is in the Bible. (2) God makes himself known to human beings since *word* means an expression of an understandable idea. (3) Human beings can grasp and respond to God's self-disclosure revelation. (4) God used human beings to record his self-revitalization so it can be shared with all the earths peoples. These faith convictions are basic to the Christian faith.

Inspired by God

Inspire means to breathe into. Paul said, "All scripture is given by inspiration of God and is profitable" (2 Timothy 3:16). Paul's word theopneustos meant "go breathed." This same thought is in 2 Peter 1:21b: "Holy men of God spake as they were moved by the Holy Ghost." Thus, the writings we call scripture stem from spirit experiences. The Holy Spirit, the sacred breath, opened the mind, heart, and soul of men. Then they wrote what they had received.

Paul said also that this kind of writing is usable for building up God's people. Peter told his people they must discern what the Spirit had said through his writers. "No prophecy of scripture is a matter of one's own interpretation" (2 Peter 1:20 RSV). One cannot claim divine authority for his own ideas, which he may read into the scripture.

People differ on the meaning of *inspired*. Some believe (1) the apostles spoke as inspired men who expressed in their own words the truths that God showed them. Others believe (2) God inspired the words the writers used. Each view has strengths and weaknesses. Opinion 1 stresses that God gave men a vital place in his self-realization. We may be assured that (a) God was the source of their message; (b) we, too, can grasp the Spirit's revelation; and (c) God can use us also to serve his spiritual purposes. Yet the view has made many wonder if all the messages were from God, or if some were men's thoughts.

Opinion 2 offers assurance that all the Bible is trustworthy so one can read it with full assurance of faith. Yet the opinion leaves some questions also. In all languages most words have more than one meaning. How can one be sure which thought the Spirit gave each word, the one I see or the one you see—or some other? What about the translators? Does the Spirit give them the exact words? If so, why do we find varying emphasis expressed when we read the same passages in different modern languages? But if not, what value did the precise words of the Hebrew, Aramaic, and Greek text provide those who read only a modern language?

People differ also on the nature of the inspired message. Some believe in "propositional revelation," that God revealed certain fixed truths or propositions about himself. Others hold that in His acts and communion with people, God revealed Himself. (See line 3 of *the Baptist Faith and Message* statement).

Whatever one believes about inspiration, we can rest on two truths: (1) Every view is a choice of faith, and no one can prove that any certain view is the "correct" one. (2) We can rest in the assurance that God is true and that His servants recorded trustworthy accounts of His self-realization. Through them our knowledge of him grows.

United Redemption Message

The Bible spans a period of more than one thousand years. Its events occurred in widely scattered lands, differing cultures, and changing historical and religious conditions. It contains many forms of literature. Yet the strand that blends this variety into unity is the message of God's purpose and way of redemption. Man is a sinner, a rebel against God, and God seeks constantly to reclaim man, to build a relationship of mutual love. This is the Bible story from beginning to end.

The many biblical writers had two things in common. They had experienced the redeeming power of God's caring love. Thus, they were part of his unique community. Its people lived with the conviction that they had a covenant relationship with the Lord (Yahweh), the living God. The covenant began with Abraham (Genesis 12:1–3) and his family. It was extended to the nation Israel (Exodus 19:1–6, 24:3–8). The Old Testament develops the meaning of life under this covenant.

The New Testament teaches that all God began to do in Israel came to its highest point in Jesus Christ. Those who belong to him are God's true covenant people. Biblical writers wrote for their fellow believers. They imparted the truths of God's nature, His standards, and His purpose for His people.

The scriptures record, interpret, and apply the meaning of God's redeeming acts. The Bible serves as the external guide for shaping the life of the continuing covenant community, the church. The Bible sets the directions for God's people to take in obedience to the Spirit's specific inner guidance. He who inspired the word continues to lead as God's people follow. Jesus's promise has proved true, "When the Spirit of truth comes, He will guide you into all the truth" (John 16:12 RSV). People who are true to the Word's authority obey the Spirit. True people of the Book are also people of the Spirit. Thus, for God's people the Bible preserves and interprets the past, the history of his community, enlightens the meaning of its present, and gives assurance of its future.

Yet love for the Bible can expose God's people to two real dangers. The first is confusing convictions about the Bible, such as theories of inspiration, with believing the Bible itself. Believing the Bible means accepting the truth of its revelations and obeying its instructions. The second danger is searching God's unfolded self-revitalization for answers to numberless factual questions that tease the curiosity. God reveals himself to bring life to those who are spiritually dead, not to satisfy human curiosity—about things past, present, or future.

The spirit inspired scriptures have one basic purpose: to call people to keep submitting their lives to Jesus Christ as the Lord, now and forever—to the glory of God the Father.

How the Books of the Bible Were Written

For more than four thousand years, God has been using every day, normal people as witnesses to his love and care. This Spirit-led witness produced the books we call the Scriptures.

Baptists had no official body of transition, at least in the sense that Catholicism uses the word. Yet tradition (history and beliefs passed on to each new generation) played a vital part in shaping the Bible. Let's consider some of the ways.

The typewriter, printing press, cheap paper, and almost unlimited publications have led many to suppose that books have always been produced as ours are. During much of the Old Testament period, only a tiny fraction of the people could read or write. Writing materials were rare and costly. Writings had a small place in the lives of agricultural people, farmers, and herdsmen. This meant that each generation carefully memorized matters vital to family or clan members such as teaching customs, ethics, and religion and taught them to their children. Similar accounts of details in the lives of warriors, judges, kings, and prophets were remembered. In Israel, all these kinds of stories were kept and told in the light of the people's faith in the Lord as their God.

Teachings Called Oral Tradition

These stories and teachings are called oral tradition. They made up a major part of the talk around meals and campfires and on all forms of family and clan assemblies. These discussions were a major means by which the Spirit led Israel to maintain, nurture, apply, and pass on their acts (1 Kings 14:19 and many others). Someone also wrote accounts of the work of some of the prophets (1 Chronicles 29:29, 2 Chronicles 12:15; 16:11). Such written records and the oral traditions must have been the primary sources of the history recounted in the Old Testament books from Genesis to Esther.

These books differ from modern history books in two major ways. First, they make no effort to record facts for facts sake are to cover all Israel's history. Second, they are books of religious faith. They weighed selected persons and events in the light of God's covenant with Israel and the way they influence the people's loyalty to their covenant God. We do not know who compiled these books or when.

Yet Jews felt these were inspired books, so they developed accounts traditions of their origins. The oldest and most influential of these accounts says that Moses wrote the first five books. Is this idea correct or not? Opinions differ sharply.

That Moses wrote is beyond reasonable question (Exodus 24:4; Numbers 33:2). That he used the first written body of Jewish law is almost certain (Nehemiah 8:14). Yet at least three truths stand out: (1) None of the first five books named Moses as the writer (the headings are traditional, not a part of the writing itself). (2) They referred to Moses in the third person suggesting someone else was telling of his acts. (3) The books contain numerous evidence of being written at a date much later than Moses's life. Read Genesis 36, particularly verse 31, and ponder what it suggests about events and time. None of the other historical books name his writer, so their worth stems from their spiritual value, not from their author's identity.

The poetic books—Job, Psalms, Proverbs, Ecclesiastes, Song of Solomon, and Lamentations—treat the same themes as the poetic works of most peoples: romantic love; the meaning, mystery, and tragedy of life; the way of full life and the ways of folly; the joys and privileges of meaningful worship; the suffering of pain and persecution; and the whole range of human emotions. The poetic writers also treated their themes in light of Israel's covenant faith in God. They saw that faith is the key to the meaning and glory of Israel's history and purpose.

Prophets: The Lord's Spokesmen and Preachers

The prophets were the Lord's spokesmen, his preachers. They addressed the immediate conditions of the people. Every message had two basic roots. The prophet was convinced that the Lord had sent him to call Israel to correct her ways and he addressed the people in the light of the covenant relationship with the Lord. All the prophets showed how Israel had failed to live by the law of covenant and called for a renewed loyalty to it.

Both Jeremiah and Ezekiel seemed to have shaped the books bearing their names. In all the others, we cannot be sure who shaped each book—the prophet himself or followers who collected his messages. By these varied writings, the Lord led in recording his self-realization to Israel and his cause to obedience.

The cultural situation of the New Testament was much different from Old Testament times. Writing and travel were much more common. Still most communication was by word of mouth. By this method, the gospel spread like wildfire. Eyewitnesses told of Jesus's acts and teachings. Those who believed relayed the good news. In that age, people trained their memories carefully and took pride in faithfulness to details. Yet variations of the original accounts began to spread. The thinning ranks of eyewitnesses made dependable written records necessary.

We have sure knowledge about only one detail of the writing of the gospels. In John, the writer stated his purpose (20:30–31). Neither in any gospel nor in Acts did the writer give his name in the body of the book or tell when or where he wrote. Nor did Matthew, Mark, or Luke tell why he wrote. All that links the gospels to these four apostolic men is tradition, and it stems from the second and third centuries. The first century gave us the books, but it gave us no information about them.

For the last 150 years, hosts of Bible students have examined these traditions. Many feel that they are valid, so they support them. Others think the tradition of apostolic authors cannot be true because of evidence drawn from the early Christian movement and from the books themselves.

But do not confuse believing the gospels with excepting extra-biblical traditions about them. Believing the gospels means no less than (1) perceiving their message of Jesus as the Christ, the Son of God; (2) accepting the truth of this message and its relationship to all of life; and (3) obeying Jesus's instructions and commands.

New Testament Letters Written to Meet Problems

The New Testament letters were like the work of the Old Testament prophets—written to meet specific problems in the lives of the people of Christ. Paul's works were personal letters, as were 1 and 2 Peter and 2 and 3 John. Jude may have been a letter to a known group, or it may have been a religious tract written in the form of a letter—a common practice of that era.

James 1:1 sounds like a letter, so many call it a sermon. Both Hebrews and 1 John are anonymous, and both are far more like sermons than letters. Both dealt with serious threats to the stability of the Christian faith.

Why did the writers not name themselves? We do not know, but we do know that they understood the problems Christians faced and had a deep concern for their people's welfare. Revelation was written as a letter to the "seven churches of Asia (the Roman province)" to encourage them to be faithful in the face of great opposition.

So all Old Testament and New Testament writings grew out of the Lord's dealings with his people. As they lived out their faith, some among them felt led to instruct, encourage, and challenge the group. Thus, the Spirit gave us the books we call Scriptures. Their aim is to lead people to live the life of faith under Jesus Christ as lord—to the glory of God the Father.

Canonization of the Bible Indicates Inspired, Authoritative Word of God

The Bible is the Christian canon, our inspired, authoritative literature. We who know Jesus Christ as Lord and Savior love the Bible because it opens the truth that is the solution to our tragic past, the base of our life in the present, and our hope for the future.

Canon is a Christian term, derived from the Greek *Kanon*, which had several meanings. "Rule" or "measuring stick" led to "recognize standard." The process of people recognizing that certain books are uniquely inspired is *canonization*. *Canonicity* means that the book is inspired, a measuring standard and guide in people's faith experience.

Our Old Testament consists of thirty-nine books: five books of law (Genesis to Deuteronomy), twelve historical books (Joshua to Esther), five poetic books (Job to the Song of Solomon), and seventeen prophetic books (Isaiah to Malachi). These books follow the makeup and order of the Greek and Latin translations of the Old Testament. The Hebrew Bible has the same contents arranged in twenty-four books. First and 2 Samuel are one book, as are 1 and 2 Kings, 1 and 2 Chronicles, and Ezra and Nehemiah. The twelve minor prophets make up one book. The twenty-four books consist of three divisions:

- The Law (Torah): the Pentateuch (five books, Genesis to Deuteronomy)
- The Prophets: eight books in two groups

  - Former Prophets: Joshua, Judges, Samuel, and Kings
  - Later Prophets: Isaiah, Jeremiah, Ezekiel, and the minor prophets

- The Writings: 11 books arranged in this order: Psalms, Proverbs, Job (poetry); the Song of Solomon, Ruth, Lamentations, Ecclesiastes, and Esther (Five Scrolls); Daniel (apocalyptic); Ezra-Nehemiah and Chronicles (history)

During most of the Old Testament period, Israel had no vital concept of "canon." The first evidence that a writing was accepted as God's word is in 2 Kings 22:8 (621 BC). The book of the law was found in the temple and led King Josiah to make sweeping religious reforms in Judah. Some historians call this book the Pentateuch, but others think it was Deuteronomy. Either way, the event began the process of Old Testament canonization.

The early stages involved no official action. People recognized books as inspired and put them to use. By the time of Ezra (about 444 BC), the Jews treated the book of the law, the Pentateuch, as the word of the Lord (Nehemiah 8–10). Ezra led the people to read the law in all synagogues in Judah. This led to the spread of education, so all might read the Torah. Thus, the law became the heartbeat of the Jews religious life.

Prophecy Died Out

During this period, prophecy died out in Israel. A popular Jewish theory said that an unbroken succession of inspired prophets extended from Moses to Ezra. Then they ceased. So no inspired book could come after Ezra's time, which Jews roughly equated with the rise of Alexander the Great. The law gave instructions for the present, but it left life incomplete. The people needed a sense of Israel's past glory and future hope. The books of the Prophets met this need as Jews began reading them in the synagogues (after 200 BC).

Thereafter, rabbis openly discussed sacred books. The Law and the Prophets (all eight books) were considered sacred, but opinions varied on later books. Jews generally accepted the books of the writings as sacred by Jesus's time. This is the only group of books on which Jews took official action to close the canon. The destruction of Jerusalem and the Christian movement forced them to set an authoritative list of sacred books. About AD 90, a council of Pharisees met at Jamnia, a village between Jerusalem and the coast. They closed this section of the Hebrew Canon, using three standards for acceptance: (1) survival for centuries (books were expensive and could not survive unless the people love them); (2) anonymity (an indication of enough age to have been written before prophecy ceased); and (3) originally written in Hebrew not in Greek, which would indicate a date after prophecy ceased. Thus, Jews limited inspiration to their canon.

Palestinian Jews also eliminated books that were part of the Septuagint, the Greek translation of the Old Testament. Christians preserved that translation, using it all over the Roman empire. It included fifteen books that appear also in the Latin translation. Catholic translations include them, but Protestant groups adopted the Hebrew Canon.

The first Christians were Jews, who inherited from Judaism a body of sacred literature but not a canon. In worship, they read from these books—Law, Prophets, and Writings—and probably the "Apocrypha" since most Christian groups read the Greek Old Testament. They also recounted the oral tradition of Jesus's words and acts, concentrating on the meaning of the resurrection.

With time, words from apostles were cited and their letters read, as well as letters from current leaders. But through the early part of the second century some debated the propriety of reading anything other than the sacred scriptures. That's the first step in forming a canon was the use of Christian books in worship before they were called sacred.

The early writers had no idea of contributing to a "New Testament." What need did they have for a new scripture? They expected Jesus to return just any day. They wrote to meet the immediate needs of the faithful. Thus, the process of New Testament canonization began unconsciously, unplanned.

Early Christians consider themselves inspired by the same spirit who inspired all the prophets. This view spawned two facts: (1) These Christians found authority in the word of the risen Lord directly available through inspiration and revelation (see Galatians 1:11–12). Thus, a high value on oral tradition prevented full acceptance of written revelation until after AD 200. (2) The view that the Spirit had inspired apostolic writers became a natural sequel.

Christian Writings Circulated

During the second century, many Christian writings circulated. We know of at least this many ancient apocryphal Christian books: twenty gospels, twenty-two "Acts," seven epistles, and six apocalypses. As these and unknown others circulated, the people's sense of writings inspired nature determined which books endured through use in worship.

The second step in forming a canon was the grouping of books. By AD 175, our Gospels had become a group and widely accepted as equal authority with the Old Testament. By AD 140, Marcion, the first prominent Gnostic, had all Paul's known letters (ten) except the pastorals (Timothy and Titus). By AD 175, all thirteen seemed to have been a collection. Of the general letters, 1 Peter and 1 John were accepted quickly but the others in Revelation were much debated.

The first step stemmed from the need for a canon caused by attacks from the outside and divisions from within the church. The rather free attitude toward inspiration forced Christians to begin limiting books accepted for use in worship. By AD 200, men defended the four Gospels as the final expression of the good news, being equal in content to the oral tradition.

Because Marcionites had tried to write in Paul's name, Paul's thirteen letters became a fixed group. An ancient manuscript, known as the Muratorian Canon, written in Rome before AD 200, listed the books accepted by the Catholic (universal) church: the four gospels; Acts, Paul's 13 letters, two Epistles of John, Jude, and Revelation, plus the Wisdom of Solomon and the Revelation of Peter. The Shepherd of Hermas, a widely read book that many accepted as inspired, was rejected because it was "written recently, in our times."

Thus, the main body of our canon was well set shortly after AD 200. But Hebrews, James, 2 Peter, 2 and 3 John, Jude, and Revelation were debated throughout the third century.

The Christian Canon

About AD 320, Eusebius, the first Greek church historian, produced a list of "spurious," "accepted," and "debated" books. Too, he stated a set of standards of canonicity that had great influence: apostolic authorship, universal acceptance, and appropriate doctrinal content.

The last step in forming the Christian canon began in AD 367. Athanasius, the bishop of Alexandria, wrote an Easter letter to his churches. In it, he listed our twenty-seven books as authoritative. By AD 400, the Latin churches accepted this list. In AD 393, the Council of Hippo (a city in North Africa) had approved the list, separating Hebrews from Paul's works. In AD 419, the council of Carthage, another city in North Africa, approved the list but put Hebrews among Paul's works.

For almost 1,700 years, Christians have read these books and affirmed that they bear the marks of the Spirit who is working in us. Yet Christians have not followed Jews in making inspiration and canon equal. We must remember that the value of the Spirit's inspiration of the Bible hinges on the Spirit's directing those who read and hear. People who are true to the book are people with the Spirit who gave the book.

Chapel Address

Dr. William Coble

November 16, 1978

Text: Colossians 1:9–11

> "And so, from the day we heard it we have not ceased to pray for you, asking that you may be filled with the knowledge of His will, and all spiritual wisdom and understanding, to lead a life worthy of the Lord, fully pleasing to him, bearing fruit in every good work and increasing in the knowledge of God. May you be strengthened with all power, according to His glorious might, for all endurance and patience with joy."

We might say that the study of the history of the human race is a tracing of the great power struggle. Modern history blends well with ancient history as we see how people, everywhere they have lived, have coveted, and grasped for power. In the New Testament a very significant and clear line is drawn. That line tells us that the use of God's power is the major dividing line between the divine and the devilish. The use of power in any other way than service for the need is viewed in the New Testament as an expression of devilishness.

This fact comes into focus very early in the synoptic gospels. Jesus come at his baptism, accepted the assignment to become a servant-Messiah. In that assignment we have the defining of the essential qualities, the nature, and the purpose of God's true people. Jesus was empowered by the Holy Spirit. He was filled to carry out the assignment that was given to him. Then he was tested. He was faced with alternatives, that according to every standard of human evaluation are far more attractive, far more practical, and far more useful. We might say that the temptation experience is the test of the willingness to use power for the purpose for which it was bestowed. After all, it is highly possible to recognize the fact that there is a great appeal in using unlimited power, particularly when we are given the opportunity to distort and deceive people, to make them instruments in our own hands. That kind of power leads to the power to manipulate. The use of power that calls upon God to allow our own choices to determine our conduct and the way in which he is to reveal himself to us, passing this on to people becomes a manipulative possibility. Manipulation is just one very short step from domination. Jesus faced the temptations to distort, to manipulate, to dominate, but he remembered the voice he was assigned to serve. He had to choose between the use of power that dominates or serves. The power that dominates destroys. It destroys not only those upon whom it is expended, it destroys those who use it. Just as surely as a bomb that blows down a wall can also blow up those who attempt to ignite it.

But the craving for the power that ultimately destroys is the great thirst of human nature. A rather interesting thing about this, the synoptic gospels tell us very clearly, is that the people who accused Jesus of working through devilish power were the ones who were craving for themselves a leader who exercised the power that destroys. They were ready to manipulate, and they were ready to accept a leader who manipulated. But Jesus refused to become a manipulating person who would enable them to become dominant. Then the finger of accusation was pointed. "You're doing what you're doing by the power of the devil."

Paul knew what it meant to have to face people who loved, craved, and operated by manipulating, dominating, devilish power. He was around that kind of people constantly because they were convinced that Paul was a distorter of the way God operates among people. The Judaizers that followed him through Galatia, Asia, and Greece were always warning people that Paul was only telling half-truths. Then came the early Gnostic thinkers who looked upon Paul's simple gospel as something that was rather childishly naive, certainly not for the "mature and understanding." He knew how pious these people sound. He knew how theologically vital they could appear. After all, these were people who were bringing the 'truths of God down to practical application' with the everyday affairs of life. He knew how effectively they argued, how well they recruited, and how well they organized. Paul knew that the struggle with the users of this kind of power was never ending. He knew this because he knew that the devil just doesn't quit.

We also face these pressures. We have become a part of a system that is perfectly willing to manipulate provided it produces visible results. We are given reasons for planning our systems in order to defend the purposes and expand the plans of God. But there is one thing that is certain. That little voice that keeps speaking to us. It keeps telling us it doesn't matter how you do things, what really matters is your purpose. Are you honoring God? Are you exalting him before his created world that is living in rebellion against him? Do whatever you have to do to honor him. That voice isn't the Holy Spirit. That voice is the same voice that was talking in the wilderness, and it kept talking through such 'experts of spiritual truth' as Simon Peter, James and John, the Scribes, and the Pharisees. That little voice keeps gaining a hearing as we live in our church life. After all, we do know something about church difficulties. The vast majority of these difficulties that we sometimes call personality conflicts are conflicts for power to dominate. The power to make decisions that shape the function and ministry of people other than ourselves is something we all have to face.

Our assignment, however, is still to be a servant. We are to be servants who operate by the power of God who gave himself, who calls upon us to give ourselves, to be willing to be used rather than to use others. As Peter put it in the second chapter of his first letter, it is to this we were called.

Peter knew ... Paul knew ... as Jesus knew that the effort to respond to that call is one that brings suffering. It brings all kinds of hardships. That is the reason why Paul was praying for the

Colossians. "Praying that you may be strengthened with all power according to his glorious might, for all endurance and patience." The operation of the power of God as Paul understood it is wrapped up in this word: the word that is translated here <u>patience</u> is one that we might describe as "the Spirit that refuses to give up." Paul knew why people would feel that it was time to just quit. He knew how cruel the world could be to witnesses that bring a sense of conviction for wrong. He knew how hard this world could make it just to get along, just to make a living. He knew how meager the responses to efforts to serve people could be. He understood that although there are so many people who feel a deep need for somebody who cares, a large number, and large proportion of mankind have no real desire for one in their midst who is a devoted servant.

Such a situation leads to meager results for one's efforts. Paul knew how meager these could be and he knew how quickly those who did respond could fall away. He knew how many that remained could very easily be led into spiritual delusions. He knew how slowly those who were faithful grew in the faith itself. All this boils down to the fact that Paul was very aware of the fact that a great amount of effort can produce mighty small results. Since the demand is so great and the results so meager, why keep on? Because that's the way the God works in people! When we consider the continued expression of the strength and power of those willing to dominate, there is something in the conflict that stirs them up on the inside. For the person who has devoted to service the only source of his continually renewed power is the Spirit of God himself, however.

It is in the gospel of John that we also see this thing expressed. The truth that meant so much to Paul is present there also. The glory of God is in the cross. That's the reason why Jesus didn't quit. That is the reason why Paul didn't quit. That is the reason why people who are filled with God's kind of power do not quit.

The other word that Paul used in this verse might be expressed as the spirit that refuses to become bitter. Paul knew the temptation to become bitter. He knew the apparent success of those that distorted the gospel. He needed to have the apparently easy success of those who did not have to bear the kind of burden that he had to bear. Paul sometimes must have wandered, "Is God really fair?" Just as sometimes we wonder, "Why is it that that some people seem to gallop through life with the best of health in the best of their circumstances while others limp through life with sickness, all kinds of tragedies besetting them, disappointments?" That can make a person bitter if you let it. Then there is the problem of fellowship. Paul knew how many people were going around in churches where he had labored hard and long that were saying "That guy isn't fit to be an apostle. He doesn't have any business claiming what he claims."

Paul lived with this awareness of which we must live. Unforeseeable and unpredictable crisis can destroy our whole game plan of life just like the crumbling of a piece of paper, leaving no evident alternatives. That can make a person bitter. Particularly when you see the progress, the rapidity, with which somebody who at least appears to be less well-endowed just goes right on. Of course, we never see what is really happening to that person, but it looks as though he is taking it easy. Paul knew one thing that enables a person to face that kind of tragedy and not be bitter. It is not Romans 8:28. It is Romans 8:29:

> "For whom he foreknew he also predestined to be conformed to the image of his Son."

Somehow, God is taking those things that can very easily make a person bitter and using those specifically in the developing of a personality in the likeness of Jesus Christ. That is the purpose of the Spirit's work. That is the meaning of the operation of the kind of power that God gives to his people. This is the reason he calls them "servants." This is the reason we have every incentive to be optimistic.

Some time ago I came across a little piece of writing, it would be a travesty on art to call it a point, but it is a testimony; it has real meaning.

> "I dreamed many dreams that never come true,
>   true,
> I've seen them vanish at dawn.
> But I've realized enough of my dreams,
> To thank God and want to dream on.
>
> I've prayed many prayers when no answer came,
>   came,
> Though I waited patiently and long.
> But answers have come to enough of my prayers,
>   prayers,
> To keep me praying on.

I've sown many seeds that fell by the way,
For the birds to feed upon.
But I've held enough golden sheaves in my
    hands,
To make me keep sowing on.

I've drained a cup of disappointment and
    pain,
And gone through many days without a
    song.
But I've sipped enough sector from the roses
    of life,
To make me want to live on."

God strengthens his people to continue in
the face of struggle. Whatever, wherever … the
assignment.

Chapel Address

Dr. William Coble

September 20, 1984

Text: John Chapter 2

One of the major emphases of the person and work of Jesus Christ is evident in the ways in which he faces mankind with paradoxes. A paradox is a statement or a truth that seems to be contrary to common sense. The experience of Jesus and his disciples at the wedding at Cana is a place where John introduced many themes that he developed through his book. It is a veritable mind of germinal ideas. But none of these ideas are more significant than the fact that he faces us with a tremendous paradox. He is the one who lifts mechanical religion out of its shackles and transforms our relationship with God to living, vibrant joy. This one who works such transformation, however, does it in a way that human reason says, "No way!" When Jesus told his mother, my time has not yet come, John introduced the development of the theme that the genuine glory of God is the cross. The way of glory is the way of the cross. The source of the joy that he gives is the sharing of his cross. And the world says, "No way!" You see, the world is obsessed with happiness. The world knows nothing of the kind of joy that is the result of the indwelling and inworking of the living God.

Jesus's final conversation with the disciples reveals that he worked on this theme from a great many angles. None is more forthright or direct than John 14. 'My purpose for you is to know genuine joy. And I'm telling you the way. You obey my commandments. There isn't any other way.' And the world responds, 'Joy through obedience that makes me deny my selfhood!? No way.'

When I came to seminary, I came with the conviction that now, for the first time in my life, I would know the meaning of real fellowship with God's people. In a place where everyone is called to the Lord's service, people will surely be living and demonstrating kindness, consideration, helpfulness, and gratitude. I haven't found it that way! From that point the stories take their unique, individual traits and almost inevitably the conclusion is "I'm just about ready to give it up! Forget it!" Disappointing expectations of maturity developed dependability in others which has led to untold measures of disappointment and tragedy within the fellowship of this body for the last 26 years.

To me that situation is well expressed in a little poem:

"The saddest thing I ever did see
Was a woodpecker pecking on a plastic tree.
He looks at me and says, 'Friend,
Things ain't as sweet as they used to be!"

I don't think there is any way to avoid the dramatic reality of that feeling. People who are looking outward for the sources of their assurance and their fulfillment in their faith in Jesus Christ, are very much like that woodpecker pecking on a plastic tree. You see, woodpeckers don't go around beating on trees just because they like to exercise their neck muscles. That's what they eat! They feed themselves. Pecking on the trees is what makes life real to them. Plastic doesn't have much of a way of gratifying even the most persevering woodpecker!

The words of the special music that was brought to us are a reminder that all the hope that we have lies not in the surroundings that we may choose very carefully and hopefully. Certainties that come to us come from a cross whereas a tragically large percentage of our day is so frequently spent listening to enticements offered by people who have no understanding of Christ's self-revelation. The sole purpose of the vast majority of the broadcasting done is to convince us that plastic is nourishing and without the proper plastic you just "ain't really living!"

The world has always been busy about this. The disciples were thoroughly convinced that their form of plastic was the full and complete expression of the will of God in the world! Their own ambitions and their own cravings, not just for wealth and power but for the opportunity to stand before an unbelieving world and say, "Look! In my hand is evidence that my faith in God is right!" Friends, that is blasphemy! Jesus took a thorough look at that whole pattern of thinking and proposing, and he rejected it totally.

Paul addressed the Philippians with such tremendous admonishment, "May you always be rejoicing in your life in the Lord, I say it again, keep on rejoicing!" This means keep on giving expression to the reasons for your joy. We are not admonished to be happy. There is no such thing as 'be happy' in Christian living. There <u>is</u> an expression of joy. The message of the cross comes back to every one of us who lives with a deep sense of limitation, and awareness of failure, the embarrassment of dreams punctured right in the presence of everybody. It comes back and says, "Look! Don't you ever forget … God made you. You are a totally unique creation. One who is usable for his purpose in a way nobody else can be." Every time we feel alone, as though this whole effort is totally worthless, we have been feeding on somebody's plastic tree!

None of us is anything other than dust. God made us this way. This was his design. Enlivened by the breathing and of his Spirit, this is what we are. This is all we have to offer. Anyone who is ashamed of having no more to offer is passing his own judgement on God's decisions. The message of the cross is our reminder. God intends for us to stand straight, whether we can stand tall or not. Sometimes we get too obsessed with height as though there is no glory in the valleys. Friends, it isn't that in the valleys that our character is shaped. The message of the cross is the reminder that ultimately what we do does depend on us. You see, the cross is the climax of the whole process of incarnation. God does make persons. He gives us personal responsibilities. Although the brilliant visions that may have led us to accept his call may seem to be fading, what he has for us to do will never fade, if we do it. With him, the issue is not "how big is the job I get?" The issue to him is "how faithful to it am I?" His measuring stick has no relationship to plastic trees.

As we think of him, remember that he came from a nothing family, a nothing town, among what the world looked upon as a nothing people … but he changed the world. This is the one you serve. Just keep on following him.

Chapel Address

Dr. William Coble

September 17, 1985

Jesus concentrated on people, not on ideas. Everywhere Jesus went he was beset with the tragedy of 'aloneness.' Human creatures, so designed in creation that they could reach their true potential only in relationships, were living amid forces that tended to separate and isolate. This left people wondering, "What is it all about?" The great tragedy is that the very religion they profess, the worship of the Lord who was creator and who had made man in his own likeness, had joined in this sense of alienation. The very covenant that was designed to bring people together to live in relationships had turned into a kind of thought, and act that only aggravated separation and isolation. The predominant force was a force of progressive separation in alienation.

This is a problem in our own time with which we are keenly familiar. This same person that spends a tremendous amount of time talking about "togetherness" (relationship has become one of the 'in' words) often does not realize that the way it is used has very little to do with the production of "oneness" between anybody.

Our whole society, far more than the Jewish society, works towards isolation. The homes where we live are being made more soundproof and more enclosed to have the proper temperature and humidity of the air inside. As a result, all contact with that which is around seems to be cut off. Advancements in computer science have made it possible for a person to conduct the whole pattern of life and never have to leave home! It is possible to run a successful business right inside that little enclave! When we do get out among people we are surrounded by an equally enclosed vehicle. Just by chance some degree of sound might penetrate, there is some kind of electronic system that guarantees it will produce enough sound to drown out the outside sounds of life. Even when people go out to walk where other people exist without a covering around them the headphones will guarantee that you will not have to bother with other people!

Isolation is in our society. But what about our faith? In our tradition there is, and has been for well over a century, a tremendous drift toward strict individualism. The only thing that matters is what is between me and God! If we have the right theological system... we become unacceptable. Separation and isolation are thus often built into the very nature of our thinking about the God who created us to be together. In our worship, if our rituals are right, we are considered to be acceptable. Separated by those very things that were designed to remind us of every time they had performed that we are a body in Christ! We are not to be isolated individuals. Even in the rules of conduct, again if we have the right rules and live by them rightly, we can be accepted. If we do not live by the right rules, then there is progressive alienation.

But Jesus still walks in our midst. As he walked among the Jews his call to them was, "Follow me!" The thing that he tried to drive home was that the call to follow is to become a "fellow." The very word fellow comes from an old English term that pictures a person who puts down some kind of money or property to be used in a joint enterprise. The word fellow means that one is involved in relationships with others. Fellowship becomes the mutual sharing of each one investing something that becomes common to all. When we cast this in the spiritual mode each one invests something uniquely of self in order that we may be genuinely one. This kind of relationship is one that's voluntarily entered. It is not the kind of tie that binds people to birthrights, legal obligations, etc. We enter it freely because we are committed to the one who has called us into living relationships. The very words that are central to our whole faith perspective are words of relationship, not words of detail.

The two words, "faith" and "agape," are words of personal relationship. In faith we perceive that which is worthy of trust in another person. Having perceived that worthiness of trust our "faith" is activated as we entrust self to that person. By faith we are called to a living relationship with Jesus Christ as the Lord of life. We make him Lord if we obey his kind of commandments. His kind of commandments focus on this other keyword, "love." I think that all of you are aware of the fact that we do not have any English word that does it justice. The best we can do is "love." But agape means a whole lot more specific reality than does our word love. Agape is that expression of genuine concern for another person that leads to self-giving. Agape, for God, means that we are devoted to him to the extent that he is the controller of life. He is the one who we do trust, who we do obey. Agape for each other means that we give ourselves for the benefit of each other.

This call comes to us in a manner that we still don't really give consideration. When Jesus said, "Follow me," he challenged us to begin living out in our sphere another edition of the incarnation. As we think of his coming, the one who was divine who became genuine flesh, he dwelt among us, and we had the privilege of seeing who and what he was. He called you and me to share that kind of experience because in Christian fellowship there are the dual roles. Every person we meet needs something we must give. Jesus Christ came into this world, not to take control of it, but to give himself for it. He calls us to follow him that we might become fishers of people, devoted to the process of bringing to other people that fullness for which God created them, for which he gave his only son. As God's agents we must become avenues of his unique kind of restorative powers.

But on the other hand, we walk among those who need what God can use us to give. As creatures of equally desperate need, we must live on the human track also. As God works through us, we must allow him to work through others for us.

Nothing is as destructive to the vitality of Christian fellowship as the feeling "I can help you, but praise God I do not really need you." I can get along without you. No! As genuine of an expression of agape is demanded to serve others, an even higher expression of the agape is demanded when we allow others to serve us. By letting others serve us, their personhood is also fulfilled. They, too, will know the glory of being a creature created in the image of God. Fellowship is a goodbye that both gives and receives. It is the Spirit that is willing to let Christ, the divine one, both use us and enable us to let him use others. This voluntary exchange of the gifts of God to enrich each other is the essence of Christian fellowship.

Might that God lift us to the point that we would truly understand what Paul said…

> If I do not have the habit of speaking in tongues, not just men's tongues but angels' tongues, and I do not practice agape, I am no more than a common pagan religious sound.
>
> Corinth heard many noisy gongs and lots of cymbals and they knew where they came from.
>
> If I have prophetic powers, and I understand all of God's revealed secrets, and I have all the knowledge, my theology being above question, and if I practice the exercise of all kinds of faith, even to remove mountains, but I do not practice agape, I am nothing. And if I give away all that I have and I give my body to be burned, and I do not practice agape, I gain nothing.

I do not believe that more serious words were ever penned, and more difficult to live by.

Chapel Address

Dr. William Coble

November 8, 1988

This morning I'm going to depart somewhat from what we might call a normal format in Chapel and go back to a dimension that was used with some frequency when I was in student work. I am asking that we engage in a brief exercise of introspection that is totally personal and individual. I would hope, by whatever means, or method that is most comfortable to you, you would try to block out the sights and sounds of our setting so that you might be free to bring some word pictures into clear focus. Let your imagination work. I want to speak directly about your selfhood and not so much about the circumstances.

There are four scenes to the picture. We hope they are subsequential. First, you are a Jew of almost 2000 years ago. You are a Jew of Judea, of the priestly bloodlines. Father and mother both can trace their lineage to Abraham and Sarah. The whole family: four sons and two daughters, are devoted Jews totally committed to the Torah. The Torah is understood to be both the written word, divinely inspired and inerrant in every sentence, word, and letter, as well as the oral traditions of elders passed through generations of faithful rabbis. Faith binds the family together as a solid unbreakable unit. You are living servants of the Lord God. Every year you all go to Jerusalem to celebrate the feast of Passover, Pentecost, and Tabernacles. As a family you're living anchors to the local synagogue and the Lord has richly rewarded such faithfulness through a very comfortable lifestyle and many loyal friends.

Second, you personally are in high standing with Jerusalem's authority figures. You're one of the Pharisees on the committee of whom the authorities depend for keeping tabs on all teachers within Judaism, particularly traveling teachers. One day you heard, for the first many reports, on a quite sensational, often radical, new traveling teacher in Galilee. Your response: "Humph! Galilee?! Must be another of the offspring of those so-called Hyracanean consulates!" When the Jews were an independent kingdom, King John Hyracanean conquered the gentile territory in Galilee and offered the living males a deal: "Pledge allegiance to the Torah by accepting circumcision or lose your head!" Converts showed up in long lines. But even under the Torah, these people remained solidly lower class, always stirring up some revolutionary movement, much inspired by those contemptible Greeks.

Your team had to check him out. So, you begin tagging along, watching and listening, taking mental notes carefully. The life was never dull! He at least seemed to do some amazing things! But most committee members assumed that it was, in all probability, trickery. Even with that attitude he kept you amazed. He was so very attractive, pleasant, gracious, and helpful to all. Although he was totally committed to God, he showed nothing of what many call "normal Jewish pride." You saw him clear persons of the control of evil spirits. He enabled paralytics to walk and blind people to see. He even brought at least three corpses to life: the daughter of one of your prominent synagogue leaders, a son of a most pitiful widow, and even your old friend, Lazarus of Bethany! And you knew he was dead!

This man called Joshua of Nazareth had an endless line of other such acts for which he never sought thanks, pay, or recognition. Yet you felt that even these deeds could not justify other things that you saw and heard. He claimed the power to forgive sins! He regularly violated the sacred laws of the Sabbath! He even healed people right in the synagogue under the committees very eyes! He associated freely with Jewish law-breakers, he went to their parties, drank their wine, ate their food, played their games! And you know, he never properly reproached those sinners for refusing to live by the Torah's high standards of personal and group purity before God! In fact, he openly displayed unconcern about such sacred matters! But even more, that man taught openly that God loves those who are cursed with great poverty! He even said, "You whom the Lord has blessed richly do not have special privilege, but special duty to share his blessed gifts with the hungry, the naked, and the helpless!" Of course, to you, he sounded as if he meant that you who have earned what has come to you should give it to those who cannot or will not earn their own, never having merited a blessing from the Lord! He even taught that unless you give generously to the poor, it is useless to go to Jerusalem to offer sacrifices to the Lord! How distorted can even a Galilean Jew be?!

You finally had the privilege of seeing him get his just desserts on a cross. But even then, some of his followers circulated what you called a vicious lie that he had been raised from the dead! How glad you were that nothing seemed to come from those reports.

The third scene: In a few weeks you went happily to Jerusalem to celebrate Pentecost, secure in the certainty of not having to see anymore or hear any more of that vile pretender. So, on the morning of that great day of the feast you went to the temple anticipating a happy celebration of that spring's bountiful harvest. But there you found that many of his followers had almost taken over the temple! With radiant joy they were telling how God had established that Joshua of Israel's Messiah by raising him from the dead! And something (they said it was God's Holy Spirit) was moving people who had come from all over the world! When those people responded to that message, they were filled with a joy that surpassed description! And you… you… found the power of their witness to be almost irresistible!

The fourth scene is very brief. You are now yourself in the seminary sanctuary of the twentieth Christian century. There are three questions to ask:

1. In comparison to the Jew who you were, to what extent is the supreme expression of your life commitment to God a fixed devotion to a written text and/or to the traditions that centuries

of authoritative teachers have handed down?

2. How do you respond to teaching that says your relationship to the living God hinges ultimately on your self-giving love for those in need whom you see around you and around the world?

3. Knowing yourself as you do, and only you know, what is the chance that the Jew who you were would have responded at last to the Holy Spirit's call at Pentecost, or later?

Chapel Address

Dr. William Coble

May 9, 1989

Text: Luke 3:3–17

I chose to deal with John the Baptist this morning, because in a sense, he presents to us examples of the great paradox. There are many supposed authorities who observed that there is nobody quite as strange as people! This expression has arisen out of life's great paradoxes. Every generation seems obsessed with the conviction: "There has never been people like us before, or a time like ours." Yet, as far back as we have knowledge of the Bible's place in the life of people, it has been established clearly that the great impact upon people has not been made by the prophets' oratory, nor the apostles' teachings, nor even the psalmist's psalms. The primary impact upon people is made by the study of the persons who embody the faith. From those who are not like us we learn the most.

John very clearly would have to be ranked as at least one of the ten most famous characters of scripture. In proportion to the amount of material devoted to his life and ministry, John has been abnormally famous. There is a reason. John, in many ways, brings to light the problem of the paradox. He provides us with information and examples alike. John showed by his ministry that he was overwhelmed with a sense of God's living presence. He called the people of his time to enter that glory.

But the people who held the keys to the formation and the experiencing of Jewish life were so busy being religious they didn't have time to listen to a message from God! It was the common people who came and heard John and rejoiced with him, not the leaders. Those leaders were busy keeping the rules. And how they kept them! They felt contempt for all who did not keep the rules. They observed feasts. Three times a year they overwhelmed Jerusalem. They made blood flow from the temple in an unbelievable torrent! They maintained and directed the synagogues and they sought to oversee the way everyone in Israel observed the law. They were busy people! They did not have a lot of time on their hands! Certainly not the kind of time that was required to go out into the wilderness to hear a man who was trying to act like Elijah. We might say that there were a lot of "busy bodies" as well as busy people! They were feeling responsible for seeing that all the circumcised were devoted to keeping the rules as they were, fed by the dream that if all of Israel would just keep all the law for one day, the Messiah would come. They had no concept nor insight that even began to suggest that the Messiah would come for any other reason. Certainly not as one who would, to a great extent, bypass their rules!

John lived with a deep conviction that God had made him an agent of Israel's fulfillment of God's purposes for Israel. John did what he did because he could do no other. He pointed Israel toward the day of divine will. John called people to the same kind of generous care for others' needs that Jesus himself proclaimed. He called particularly for generosity to people. After all, John walked with the God who kept trying to show the world the only real value in this world is life.

Formalities are essentially insignificant. Particularly are they insignificant when they take the place of priority over persons. There were words of people within Judea, Galilee, Samaria, and Berea who didn't have fit clothes to wear. There was a tremendous number of people who never really knew what it meant to have a full stomach. They knew the pangs of hunger. To these, John extended the hand of mercy. 'Care for these in need if you would be the servants of God.' The issue of God-man relationships is not a matter of observing religious forms of any kind. The issue is caring for people at the point of their particular need.

To be godly people, those who have must take the initiative. For those in need the choice is the choice between begging and stealing. One destroys one's reputation and the other destroys one's sense of one's own being. God's care for persons takes in the whole person. John said, "You treat the needy as you would wish to be treated if your roles were reversed." That is a reasonably practical guide. John insisted that personal response to needs if the life-pattern that leads people along the path to God's will and its fulfillment. Following that path will lead to the fulfillment that God plans: the coming of the one whom they thought they wanted so badly!

Israel could not see their glory in the future by way of self-giving service. They lived in a constant dream of their own. 'Our glory stems ultimately out of our past. After all, we are the children of Abraham! And God has promised we shall inherit the earth.' John sought to jar the mind of Israel out of the past into the present in order that the future might take the shape God had for it. People who feel that their future is secure whatever happens find little reason to spend much time or energy on the common affairs of daily life. There are a few exceptions because those exceptions have learned what it means to walk with God.

John's faith in God proved to be dangerous. The people whom he addressed wanted only peace and prosperity. We can best gain a perspective of an era of history when we learn how it shaped and challenged the lives of the strong and the evils it produced in the weak. John did not think that Herod's being ruler of Galilee put him above the scriptures' stated standards of marriage in the life of God's people. So, John openly stated the case, and a 'lady' was embarrassed. John landed in prison, then finally at her request, John lost his head to the executioner's blade. Faith in the living God almost always becomes dangerous for people who feel it leading them to obey God. The fulfillment of the story of Genesis 3 appears in the fact that when people demonstrate by their lives that their habit is to obey God, some way or another they get into trouble.

One of the great paradoxes of our own age grows distinctly out of the proclaimed standard: "Be true to the Bible." From Matthew 1 to the end of Revelation 22, the message reminds us, the only thing more dangerous than being true to the message of life is refusal to be true to it. We are now in a dilemma. How does one truly proclaim God's call and challenge? How can we appeal to people to follow a dangerous life pattern? When the controlling atmosphere demands that every aspect of the gospel be stated in terms of the complete, absolute, personal security of all whose bodies have stirred the baptismal waters. Somehow or another the sense of security and the willingness to accept danger just do not fit!

The ultimate decision is rather simple to state: "Is my, or your faith stable and committed, as was John's faith?" or "Is my or your faith as adjustable to the circumstances as was the faith of Herod?" The choice is ours. Choosing faith is also choosing the results. You see, Jesus went far out of his way to impress honest people that he called them to walk with danger.

Chapel Address

Dr. William Coble

November 16, 1978

Text: Colossians 1:9–11

"And so, from the day we heard it we have not ceased to pray for you, asking that you may be filled with the knowledge of his will, and all spiritual wisdom and understanding, to lead a life worthy of the Lord, fully pleasing to him, bearing fruit in every good work and increasing in the knowledge of God. May you be strengthened with all power, according to his glorious might, for all endurance and patience with joy."

We might say that the study of the history of humans is a tracing of the great power struggle. Modern history blends well with ancient history as we see how people, everywhere they have lived, have coveted, and grasped for power. In the New Testament a very significant and clear line is drawn. That line tells us that the use of God's power is the major dividing line between the divine and the devilish. The use of power in any other way than service for the need is viewed in the New Testament as an expression of devilishness.

This fact comes into focus very early in the synoptic gospels. Jesus, at his baptism, accepted the assignment to become a servant-messiah. In that assignment we have the defining of the essential qualities, the nature, and the purpose of God's true people. Jesus was empowered by the Holy Spirit. He was filled to carry out the assignment that was given to him. Then he was tested. He was faced with alternatives, that according to every standard of human evaluation, are far more attractive, far more practical, and far more useful. We might say that the temptation experience is a test of the willingness to use power for the purpose for which it was bestowed. After all, it is highly possible to recognize the fact that there is a great appeal in using unlimited power, particularly when we are given the opportunity to distort and deceive people, to make them instruments in our own hands. That kind of power leads to the power to manipulate. The use of power that calls upon God to allow our own choices to determine our conduct and the way in which he is to reveal himself to us, passing this on to people becomes a manipulative possibility. Manipulation is just one very short step from domination. Jesus faced the temptations to distort, to manipulate, to dominate, but he remembered the voice he was assigned to serve. He had to choose between a use of power that dominates or serves. The power that dominates destroys. It destroys not only those upon whom it is suspended, it destroys those who use it. Just as surely as a bomb that blows down a wall can also blow up those who attempt to ignite it.

But the craving for the power that ultimately destroys is the great thirst of human nature. A rather interesting thing about this, the synoptic gospels tell us very clearly, is that the people who accused Jesus of working through devilish power were the ones who were craving for themselves a leader who exercised the power that destroys. They were ready to manipulate, and they were ready to accept a leader who manipulated. But Jesus refused to become a manipulating person who would enable them to become dominant. Then the finger of accusation was pointed. "You're doing what you're doing by the power of the devil!"

Paul knew what it meant to have to face people who love, crave, and operate by manipulating, dominating, devilish power. He was around that kind of people constantly because they were convinced that Paul was a distorter of the way God operates among people. The Judaizers that followed him through Galatia, Asia, and Greece were always warning people that Paul was only telling half-truths. Then came the early Gnostic thinkers who looked upon Paul's simple gospel as something that was rather childishly naive, certainly not for the mature and understanding. He knew how pious these people sound. He knew how theologically vital they could appear. After all, these were the people who were bringing the truth of God down to practical application with the everyday affairs of life. He knew how effectively they argued, how well they recruited, and how well they organized. Paul knew that the struggle with the users of this kind of power is never-ending. He knew this because he knew that the devil just doesn't quit.

We also face these pressures. We have become part of a system that is perfectly willing to manipulate provided it produces visible results. We are given reasons for planning our systems to defend the purposes and expand the plans of God. But there is one thing that is certain. That little voice that keeps speaking to us. It keeps telling us "It doesn't matter how you do things, what really matters is your purpose." Are you honoring God? Are you exalting him before his creative world that is living in rebellion against him? Do whatever you have to do to honor him. That voice isn't the Holy Spirit. That voice is the same voice that was talking in the wilderness, and it kept talking through such experts of spiritual truth as Simon Peter, James, and John, the Scribes, and the Pharisees. That little voice keeps gaining a hearing as we live in our church life. After all, we do know something about church difficulties. Most of these difficulties that we sometimes call personality conflicts are conflicts for power to dominate! The power to make decisions that shape the function and ministry of people other than us is something we all must face.

Our assignment, however, is still to be a servant. We are to be servants who operate by the power of a God who gave himself, who calls upon us to give ourselves, to be willing to be used rather than to use others. As Peter put it in the second chapter of his first letter, "It is to this we were called."

Peter knew… Paul knew… as Jesus knew, that the effort to respond to that call is one that brings suffering. It brings all kinds of hardships. That is the reason why Paul was praying for the

Colossians. "Praying that you may be strengthened with all power according to his glorious might, for all endurance and patience." The operation of the power of God as Paul understood it is wrapped up in this word: the word that is translated here patience is one that we might describe as "the spirit that refuses to give up." Paul knew why people would feel that it was time to just quit. He knew how cruel the world could be to witnesses that bring a sense of conviction for wrong. He knew how hard this world could make it just to get along, just to make a living. He knew how meager the responses to efforts to serve people could be. He understood that, although there are so many people who feel a need for somebody who cares, a large number, a large portion of mankind have no real desire for one in their midst who is a devoted servant.

Such a situation leads to meager results for one's efforts. Paul knew how meager these could be and he knew how quickly those who did respond could fall away. He knew how many that remained could very easily be led into spiritual delusions. He knew how slowly those who were faithful grew in the faith itself. All this boils down to the fact that Paul is very aware of the fact that a great amount of effort can produce mighty small results. Since the demand is so great and the results so meager, why keep on? Because that's the way God works in people! When we consider the continued expression of the strength and power of those willing to dominate, there is something in the conflict that stirs them up on the inside. For the person who is devoted to service the only source of his continually renewed power is the Spirit of God himself, however.

It is in the gospel of John that we also see this thing expressed. The truth that meant so much to Paul was present there also. The glory of God is in the cross. That's the reason why Jesus didn't quit. That is the reason why Paul didn't quit. That is the reason why people who are filled with God's kind of power do not quit.

The other word that Paul used in this verse might be expressed as "the spirit that refuses to become bitter." Paul knew the temptation to become bitter. He knew the apparent success of those that distorted the gospel. He knew of the apparently easy success of those who did not have to bear the kind of burden that he had to bear. Paul sometimes must have wondered, "Is God really fair?" Just as sometimes we wonder, "Why is it that some people seem to gallop through life with the best of health and the best of circumstances while others limp through life with sickness, all kinds of tragedies besetting them, disappointments?" That can make a person bitter if you will let it. Then there is the problem of fellowship. Paul knew how many people were going around in churches where he had labored hard and long that were saying "That guy isn't fit to be an apostle. He doesn't have any business claiming what he claims."

Paul lived with this awareness of which we must live. Unforeseeable and unpredictable crisis can destroy our whole game plan of life just like the crumbling of a piece of paper, leaving no evident alternatives. That could make a person bitter. Particularly when you see the progress, the rapidity, with which somebody who at least appears to be less well-endowed just goes right on. Of course, we never see what is really happening to that person, but it looks as though he is taking it easy. Only have one thing that enables a person to face that kind of tragedy and not be bitter. It is not Romans 8:28. It is Romans 8:29:

"For whom he foreknew he also predestined to be conformed to the image of his Son."

Somehow, God is taking those things that can very easily make a person bitter and using them specifically in the developing of a personality in the likeness of Jesus Christ. That is the purpose of the Spirit's work. That is the meaning of the operation of the kind of power that God gives to his people. This is the reason he calls them "servants." This is the reason we have every incentive to be optimistic.

Some time ago I came across a little piece of writing, it would be a travesty on art to call it a poem, but it is a testimony; it has real meaning.

"I've dreamed many dreams that never came
    true,
I've seen them vanish at dawn.
But I've realized enough of my dreams,
To thank God and want to dream on.

I've prayed many prayers when no answer
    came,
Though I waited patiently and long.
But answers have come to enough of my
    prayers,
To keep me praying on.

I've sown many seeds that fell by the way,
For the birds to feed upon.

But I've held enough golden sheaves in my
        hands,
To make me keep sowing on.

I've drained a cup of disappointment and
        pain,
And gone many days without a song.
But I've sipped enough nectar from the
        roses of life,
To make me want to live on."

God strengthens his people to continue in
the face of struggle. Whatever, wherever… the
assignment.

Convocation Address
Presented at Fall Convocation of Midwestern Baptist Theological Seminary

By Dr. William Coble

September 6, 1966

In preparing a paper of this type obviously the most difficult choice to make is the selection of a subject. Several interesting and worthwhile areas are open, some old—such as the Dead Sea Scrolls and Bultmann, some new—the new hermeneutic and several theological, moral, and critical problems arising out of the space age. So, there are ample ways by which the subject of the believer's security could have been avoided honorably. But it needs discussion because it is a way of coming to grips with ourselves. It is now a problem of great dimensions in Baptist circles because it is symptomatic of our people's total relation to Christ. When highly insecure people suspect someone of tampering with the source of what security they do have, they agitate easily; so, its emotional potential is second only to that of the problem of race relations. Yet if we are not willing to face the issues of our day, there's no justification for our existence as preachers or educators. A thorough examination, however, would require such a lengthy writing that we would be here even a lot longer than this hour will seem to be; so, the purpose of this paper is not to give a detailed treatment of the general subject. It shall seek only to focus on a condition amid which we Baptist ministers do live and must serve, all in the hope that some may be stimulated to further examination of the field as a means of serving the people to whom most of us owe our spiritual existence. My only fear is that in such a discussion brevity can easily lead to misunderstanding, just as verbosity can produce boredom; but if it will stimulate real study—rather than mere heated argument—even that will be a blessing.

One must also choose whom he considers to be the primary audience, which includes the selection of style and manner of address as well. I shall be trying to address the field workers, pastoral and educational, present, and future; because they, more than any others, must deal constantly with the expressions and implications of both the problems and the glories which will be mentioned today. So, this paper is more sermonic than scholarly in the traditional sense.

When Southern Baptists are discussed, several things must be remembered. First, as Baptists we are talking, in part, about ourselves. What Paul said about the husband-wife relationship in Ephesians 5:29, applies here: "No man hates his own flesh." Too, these are people to whom all of us here are deeply indebted; so, they should be examined through the charitable eyes of gratitude. However, we may feel toward them, Southern Baptists present a varied subject of discussion. Because of almost anything one might say numerous specific opposites could be signed. So, what one sees and says may well be determined by what he seeks. Doctor J. P. Allen once said, "The worst of all lies is to generalize." Still, enough characteristics are found to be common among Baptists that one can be fair in some generalizing.

There is much good in Baptist life, which can be pointed out with thankfulness. There are many ways in which we may be called a successful denomination as our numbers grow and our work of all types expands. These achievements are not accidental but are the results of the efforts of multitudes of people who are dedicated to Christ. Church members are following the guidance of increasingly able leadership in both the local churches and all phases of denominational organization. This, coupled with the rising level of education in every area of Baptist life, has resulted in work which is better organized. The corresponding prosperity of the membership has made possible a continuous expansion and intensification of efforts to bring the message of Christ to all the world. These things are all expressive of the acceptance of life standards, which are centered in the Bible and the serious desire to carry them out.

As surely as there are those who can see nothing but good in Baptist life, there are those who see nothing but bad, and this is unfortunate. Still, it is by no means true that everyone who sees undesirable traits developing is disloyal or antagonistic. Jeremiah certainly had no less love for Judah than did Hananiah and other prophets of his stripe. From Patmos John praised the churches at Ephesus, Pergamum, and Thyatira;

then to each of them, he said, "But I have something against you." In Judea's wilderness the Baptist's message to the Lord's people was, "repent!" It is one thing to criticize, to vent one's spleen. It is another way to point out the truth with the hope that it will help to bring about the correction of errors.

Today, not all is well within our denomination. Many essentially spiritual problems appear constantly. Pride manifests itself to the degree that, in ways quite reflective of their political counterparts, our conventions are filled with reminders of our own greatness. Hate is shown in various forms: animosity toward fellow Baptists, contempt for Christians of other faiths, and indifference to the world, especially to those who are needy. Greed is a barrier to effective fellowship, individuals seeking personal prominence, just as institutions seek financial support—at the expense of others. In its own way each of these denies in life the faith which we proclaim.

Many of our practices, however, openly deny our doctrines. One such problem is compulsive activism. We preach salvation by God's grace through man's faith which results in a life of good (that is, redemptive) works. Yet a major part of our total religious life is composed of activities which our academic circles would call "busy work," doing religious things just to be sure that we are not idle. Does this suggest a sneaky suspicion that it is not really God's grace but our own achievements that save?

Another problem is institutionalism. We teach that the supreme value is human life—the individual as well as the group. To save even one life God was willing to sacrifice Heaven's supreme

Presence. Yet when the personal values of human needs cry out for someone to take up his cross, the investment in the institution—the pressure of making monthly bank note payments on everything from the church buildings to printing presses and stethoscopes—forces us into tactful silence and shameful inaction. This situation in Christendom caused George Bernard Shaw to say in the preface to his play <u>Androcles and the Lion</u>, "Barrabas has stolen his (Jesus') name and taken his cross as a standard."

We also encounter the problem of monasticism, although better terms might be isolationism or individualism. While heralding to the world that God has commanded us to go into the uttermost part of its domain, our energies are devoted more and more to the winning and preserving of our own, and the world is less and less invaded by those who carry in their person the loving power of God's redemption. "Me and mine" is so much our theme that the stirring of missionary impulse within the laity is becoming an almost impossible task.

The great backdrop from all of this is the problem of pessimism. A centuries old Baptist distinctive has been insistent upon the competence of the individual in matters of religion recognizing that there are varieties of experiences. This means that God can be trusted to reveal himself understandably and meaningfully and that man is considered capable of grasping that revelation and applying it appropriately to his life. It means that although no one of us is dependent upon the competence of someone else to serve as his priest, each of us can learn from him; then we all can profit from each other's experience. At the present, Baptist life is characterized by few things as powerful as its doubt of any form of deviation from a recognized norm. Unless one speaks in the cliches handed down from our elders, he is suspect, possibly dangerous. Even worse is anyone who might suggest a truth which involves going beyond the fixed traditions, even though Jesus did say in John 16:13 that the Holy Spirit will keep on leading us into all the truth.

To illustrate this pessimism, Baptist's claim to believe that the scriptures are God's Word, unshakable, unchangeable, the eternally valid authority which is bonding upon all and by which all will be judged. Yet if someone raises a question about the nature of the Bible's authority or suggests alternate interpretations to the traditionally accepted, we see pennants of seismographic proportion—as though some mere man could topple or even challenge that which is genuinely eternal. Then modern men become guilty of the sin of Uzzah, who sought to protect the ark of God when it seemed to be endangered by the stumbling of the oxen which pulled the cart on which it rode (II Samuel 6:6F). If we really believed that it's God's Word to man, we would know it will stand without the puny props with which men often seek to support it.

All these problems may be summed up in one term, self-centeredness. We do echo Jesus' insistence that to be a disciple one must deny self and bear his own cross—that is, the instrument on which the disciples own world totally rejects and condemns him. "Except a grain of wheat falls to the earth and die" (John 12:24) are words easy to repeat. Yet in practice we are far more concerned with saving our lives in this world than we are with losing them. We are preoccupied with our own spiritual experiences as opposed to meeting the demanding challenges of our day, through which alone God enables any disciple to bear a cross. That God's purpose might be furthered to the sacrifice of ourselves as an entire denomination seems to be a thought totally incomprehensible to our mind. Some feel that if anything should happen to Southern Baptists, the cause of Christ in this world would be totally lost. Bowing to Jezebel's Baal was no more gross idolatry! Until we show our awareness of our own expendability, our lives mock our preachments.

Yet probably the most damning of all our problems is that of simple respectability. Since the early days of Rhode Island and Virginia, Baptists have voiced the call of the scriptures, "Be ye separate." Unless they are separate, God's people can never fulfill their appointed function; because they are His instrument for bringing the total community under the Holy Spirit's conviction (John 16:7–11). Although it varies in some areas, for the most part southern Baptists are but one finger in the broad hand of American culture—no longer a separated people. Instead of being leavening, we have become a part of the flour. Instead of our continuing to live, as we broadcast, as "the people of the book," we have contributed to making the Bible just another book of the people; for it is commonplace to find local customs determining personal, moral, and social patterns about dislike, with the Bible being used to sanctify them. The scripture is no longer primarily an instrument for establishing standards of right for God's people and convicting sinful men of God's judgment but is commonly an instrument for defending the sinful practices and attitudes of men, often in the name of good Americanism, as glib interpreters select isolated passages to prove what they and their people are doing by choice is exactly what God would have them do. So, it may be said that it is in relation to the Bible that we find a key to both our virtues and our faults as a denomination, and the words of Jesus become very pertinent, "Ye search the scriptures because you think that in them you have eternal life, but it is these that bear witness of me" (John 5:39).

These situations are expressions of the terrible spiritual dearth and the mist of which we live. As we view them, there are encouraging signs. Many of our people are aware of them and are deeply concerned that we find the way out, or better stated, that we allow God to lead us out of them. Many others of our bodies sense that something is missing, that for some reason or other something is lacking or that things are not matching the ideals which are so obvious in the scriptures. Although they may be too spiritually immature to pinpoint the problem, they sorely wish things were different because what they are doing brings so little real satisfaction. On the other hand, there are at least two discouraging factors. One is at the point of leadership: many leaders are convinced that there is nothing at all wrong with what we are doing except that there needs to be more of it. Intensified effort, a shot of adrenaline, is the only approach to our situation that they can suggest. The other is that horde of people who are both unaware of anything amiss and completely unconcerned about any improvement. Whether the encouraging or the discouraging signs will be the stronger in the future, only God himself knows.

Clear story of significant spiritual movements in Christendom is that they are marked by at least three qualities: (1) The consciousness of the participants that they are involved in a deep personal experience with God, (2) A sense of purpose in relation to God and his work in man's life, instilling a willingness to make real sacrifices for the cause of Christ, and (3) A sense of surging and abiding joy. Some Baptist individuals and groups are marked by these qualities; but they are the outstanding exception, rather than the rule. Why have testimony meetings, which can do so much to heighten the spiritual tone of a congregation, become a thing of the past for most churches? This is not hard to answer: who has anything fresh to say? Our people have learned how much less is demanded of them to devotionalize and exhort than to testify. Then, to find the level of the Baptist sense of purpose in living for Christ one needs only to try to promote such things as personal witnessing, shut-in visitation, adult time spent in working with wayward youth, or therapy groups for those with marriage problems, personal frustrations, or deep-seated needs for love and attention. We are a people who want only to receive because we have so little that we can or are willing to give. As for joy in the life of our people, the one who seeks the height of incongruity will easily find it if he watches from the rostrum as the Baptist congregation sings "All Hail the Power of Jesus' Name." By the time they get to the line "Let angels prostrate fall," it's difficult to avoid the feeling that the thing most likely to happen is the collapse of the congregation. The main reason that someone who gets excited in a worship experience is so unwelcome is that he makes people aware that they do not have what he has. Of course, the addition of excitement itself is not necessarily a contribution to worship. As much as may be said about the movements for speaking in tongues today, with its Corinth-type errors and problems, we must recognize that these people are earnestly desirous that their worship experience have some reality to it. The tragedy is that if our people are satisfied to settle for things as they are, there can be little hope of improvement in our situation.

When spiritual movements lose their vitality, it is commonplace for them to seek to perpetuate themselves or preserve their identity by at least one or two methods: (1) multiply their investments in their rejection of buildings and maintaining the institutions connected with them, or (2) seek to validate their faith by an appeal to some external authority. There is real danger that to the multitudes of Baptists that the Bible has become the external authority by which they can validate a faith which has lost its power in their life.

Also, when spiritual movements lose their vitality, they tend to become completely identified with the culture during which they live, to which we have already referred. For Baptists this becomes highly significant in the light of truth which has been recognized by many and stated well by John Crocker:

> Americans more than most people in the history of mankind are obsessed with the idea of security. They set a higher premium

on safety and survival than most people who have ever lived. The result is that as a people they swing violently between the poles of complacency and hysteria.[1]

It is not too gross a generalization to say that when Baptists were (and in some places now are) struggling to be current examples of the living Christ in their community, the Lord's keeping presence was no matter of theory but one of living fellowship. As their religion became largely a matter of participating in their own kind of forms, their standing with God became a matter of almost philosophical theory, therefore one of uncertainty. This has produced a people far more fretted and worried about themselves than concern for Christ in the world for which he died. It is my conviction that to about the same degree that American people are obsessed with personal and national security, Baptists are obsessed with the doctrine of the security of the believer. A simple truth of life is that he who is secure is not particularly concerned about the matter. The more concerned one becomes, the more he reveals the depth of his own insecurity.

There is a direct connection between many of the problems and worries being experienced in our church life and the current emphasis on preaching, particularly our evangelistic message. For the most part these are difficult to outline briefly: as a sinner something is tragically wrong with man's inner nature; so, his actions violate

---

[1] John Crocker, "Decision and the Gospel," *Education for Decision*, ed. Frank E. Gaebelein, Earl G. Harrison Jr., and William L. Swing (New York: The Seabury Press, 1963), 57.

God's standards. This brings God's condemnation, which is a separation from Him now and eternal punishment in hell. Although man has never been able to alter his situation, God can. His love caused him to send his only Son into the world to meet man's need by giving himself in death by crucifixion. His victory over sin which slew him was complete, however, in that he rose again from the grave and ascended in glory into heaven where he intercedes for men. If one believes in him, accepts him by faith as his savior, he experiences a change of nature by being made a son (child) of God and is safe from his sins, granted the wondrous gift of eternal life.

This is all biblically based on thought and terminology. The trouble is that while biblical words are used, new meanings have been given to them, and the result is more disastrous to the biblical message than using totally different words might be. To many modern Baptists "sin" has become something naughty in which one indulges himself, like sipping a Schlitz, matching for cokes, or attending a ball game when there's a meeting at the church; and God is the petty kind of tyrant who becomes angry at such foibles of man. The death of Christ becomes a sort of heaven-maneuvered gimmick by which God who is alternately angry and benign can be nice to those who upset him, and still save face. "Faith" means giving an open statement of mental assent to some religious absolutes, even though they may seem so obviously false or irrelevant that they are repulsive to one's intelligence. One college student put it thus: "Faith seems to mean that one believes what he knows isn't true; and if this is the price one has to pay to go to heaven, I wonder if heaven is the kind of place, it would be worth it. "Salvation" and "eternal life" have come to mean that when one dies, he has no hell to fear but the glories of heaven to experience. To show that he is worthy of such a blessing he must be nice, go to church, and eliminate from his life such wrongs as were listed immediately above.

If anything has been demonstrated, is that this kind of message is totally lacking in the personal, emotional impact for causes one to rise above the society around him and demonstrate the spirit of militant triumph over it which has marked Christians of many ages. Of course, the picture may be overdrawn; but if it is, it is a caricature. It is not a false creation! It is no wonder that people with this general impression of what the gospel is are subject to the problems which have been described and are really disturbed over their present relationship to God, and their future hope.

The great problem concerning the security of the believer in Christ is, by many, reduced to its simplest terms, once one is saved, is he always saved? Is Christian salvation experience of such nature that, once one says that he believes in Christ, he is absolutely assured of the heavenly home? Can one climb every step of heaven's stairway but the last one, and then fall off? Through centuries this question has been argued, those on each side renouncing, denouncing, and condemning those on the other with such revulsion that we are left to wonder if any of them have read Jesus' words, "By this shall all men know that you are my disciples, if you have love for one another" (John 13:35).

The most common method of presenting either side of this discussion, particularly from the pulpit, has been the proof-text method. In this battle each side has plenty of ammunition. Baptists generally joined those with Calvinistic leanings and quote heavily from Johannine writings, particularly John 5:24, "Truly, truly, I say to you, he who hears my word, and believes Him who sent Me, has eternal life, and does not come into judgment, but has passed out of death into life;" or John 10:27–30, "My sheep shall hear My voice, and I know them, and they follow Me; and I give eternal life to them; and they shall never perish, and no one shall snatch them out of my hand. My Father, who has given them to Me, is greater than all; and no one is able to snatch them out of the Father's hand. I and the Father are one." Paul is often cited, particularly his hymn of praise in Romans 8:35, 38f, "Who shall separate us from the love of Christ? Shall tribulation or distress, or persecution, or famine, or nakedness, or peril, or sword? … I am convinced that neither death nor life, nor angels, nor principalities, nor things present nor things to come, nor powers, nor heights, nor depth, nor any other creative thing, shall be able to separate us from the love of God, which is in our Christ Jesus our Lord." I Peter 1:3–5 is frequently heard: "Blessed be the God and Father of our Lord Jesus Christ, who according to his great mercy has caused us to be born again to a living hope through the resurrection of Jesus Christ from the dead, to obtain an inheritance which is imperishable and undefiled and will not fade away, reserved in heaven for you, who are protected by the power of God through faith for a salvation ready to be revealed in the last time. Few are used more than Hebrew 7:25: "Hence also He is able to save forever those who draw near to God through Him, since He always lives to make intercession for them. These are only examples of many which are used, but they are sufficient to illustrate that the New Testament provides a solid basis for teaching that the believer is secure in the Lord.

Armenians respond by citing the warning to Christians with which the New Testament abounds. Again, we quote only enough to show the line of thought. Jesus said, "And you will be hated by all on account of my name, but it is the one who has endured to the end who will be saved … everyone therefore who should confess me before men, I will also confess him before my Father who is in heaven. But whosoever shall deny me before man, I will also deny him before my Father who is in heaven" (Matthew 10:22, 32f). Paul appealed to the Ephesians (4:30), "Do not grieve the Holy Spirit of God, by whom you are sealed for the day of redemption;" and warned Timothy, "It is a trustworthy statement: For if we died with Him, we shall also live with Him; if we endure, we shall also reign with Him; if we deny Him, he will deny us" (II Timothy 2:11fF). The book of Hebrews is heavily used because of its 303 total verses, 160 verses are hortatory, seeking by every means to remind the readers that nothing is more dangerous for a Christian than so to presume upon his own standing with God that he becomes indifferent to the demands of discipleship.

In facing this set of contrasting quotations, buttressed by others from all sections of the scriptures, the average Christian is often left in the state of hopeless confusion. For the most part both the promises and the warnings are stated in simple, forthright language; and the two sets of scriptures are beyond logical harmonizing for the average bible student; so, it seems that he must accept one or the other. If he accepts the promises of assurance, there seems to be no reasonable way to doubt that God has so ordered things that one's salvation can never be really endangered. Then what is the significance of the warnings? How can one feel threatened or motivated to greater caution in any area where he knows that he is absolutely beyond harm? But then if he takes the warning at face value, how can there be any peace in his heart about his own condition, when he knows how far his life misses the ideal of Christ? Either way one goes, he seems to be forced to decide for himself which part of the Bible is canonical, to be accepted at face value, and which is to be rejected or at least subjected to some clever footwork in interpretation.

Of course, detailed exegetical study can eliminate many differences which are far more apparent than real. To do some of this here is highly tempting, but time prevents it. The problem of such study is that it may become a way of hunting for the pattern of a forest by studying leaves and branches. It is possibly effective, ultimately, but it is very tedious.

So, we are left with the question: Just which of these two areas of emphasis is the truth? Must we choose? No! Both are the truth. Both come from the same Bible, and both speak directly to the experience which Christ gives; so, it is not "either… or" but both… and." To perceive their relationship, one must seek to rise above leaves and branches and survey the scope and contours of the forest. Along with the method of detailed analysis and exegesis the Bible must be studied as a whole, seeing passages, separate books, even the entire Bible as a unit, not just assembled small and possibly unrelated parts.

When this is done, one of the first and most important facts to become evident is that the total biblical revolution involves the principle which is at the heart of our existence. It is one of the many and deeply meaningful analogies to spiritual experiences found in the realm of electricity magnetism. It has been called "polarity." This means that there is a unit composed of two parts (poles) of like nature but of directly opposite function. They are completely interrelated and totally dependent upon each other; so, this must not be confused with dualism, which sees two separate or maybe opposite forces at work, whether independently, cooperatively, or in conflict. In polarity the unit can exist only as the two poles function in relation to each other, for the absence of either nullifies the function of the other. So, we must see that is not a fifty-fifty matter but one in which 100 and 100 or so fused that they become a new kind of 100. The clearest example of this is a simple permanent magnet, of which the earth itself is the greatest illustration, or any electrical system, particularly the battery. The two poles functioning together produce the power that is active or a tension which provides a spring of action. This is the way in which polarity differs from paradox, which merely recognizes the existence of two seemingly self-contradictory truths. Paradox is inert; polarity produces power.

Several expressions of this are vital to biblical revelation and are involved in our subject. The nature of man is one. Is man flesh or spirit, body or soul? It is not either… or, for he is both. The Bible's doctrine of man is an amplification of the truth expressed in Genesis 2:7 (RSV), "The Lord God formed man of dust from the ground and breathed into his nostrils the breath of life; and man became a living being." So, flesh and spirit are not two distinct parts into which man could be separated, because in every aspect of his being he is 100 percent flesh and 100 percent spirit. That he is both flesh and spirit makes him the living being which he is. Without either, he would be nothing.

Another is God-man relations. Is God sovereign or is man free? Logically, if either is true, the other cannot be. Yet both are true. God is sovereign in the order which he has created, and man is free in the nature and setting of which he finds himself. This means that both the sovereignty and the freedom are in a sense limited; that limitation, however, is but the expression of the nature of the order in which the whole relationship transpires, not the result of some tripping out circumstances within that order. These two poles of reality provide the dynamic of man's life under God.

The application of polarity comes to a climax at the point of our emphasis today, the nature of the experience of human redemption. Is this experience the outgrowth of something which God does, or which man does? We all know that it does not result from the action of either one but of both. It is at this point that the old Calvinistic—Armenian arguments become utterly ludicrous. The Calvinist bellows "Salvation is God's achievement," and almost under his breath, "as man receives it." The Armenian roars, "In salvation man appropriates," then he whispers, "what God has provided for all." Each system recognizes that both God and man are involved in the experience but insists upon making one primary and the other secondary. In defending their case, the hyper-advocates of both sides practically eliminate even the secondary role, to all intents and purposes, making salvation a unilateral act—of God on one hand, or of man on the other. This makes comprehension of the true experience impossible.

The fact of divine initiative is the heart of the biblical message to man. In Christ God has demonstrated his favoring concern for the welfare of his rebellious creatures, and the Bible calls it grace. Invariably the passages which speak of assurance are those which deal with that which God has done. This is finished, complete; and the results are certain. It is natural that anyone who's religious thought is concentrated upon the nature of God and his work in the world would be inclined to see the whole matter of salvation from the viewpoint of this finality, as though it were a unilateral act.

Yet even in the experience of Christ there was no unilateral action on the part of a despotic God. The sacrifice of the cross became a reality only when the Son chose to follow the path which he realized to be his Father's will. So, it is in man's redemption. God's offer of grace becomes a power operative in man only when it is, in electrical terms, "grounded" by man's response of faith. This response is the condition to which the sovereign God has seen fit to limit his own action. Man's response is free, and it is variable. The New Testament's warning passages are found in contexts which treat man's part in the experience of his own redemption. At no point in the New Testament is it assumed that man's response is fixed or final; it is treated as a possible variable, the condition under which the unvarying power of God can be released into the life of his creature. Many of the problems of understanding redemption and security have arisen from our efforts to take the finality and the certainty which characterize God's work in redemption and apply them to the part played by man. This we cannot do if we follow the New Testament.

This is the thing which makes it so essential that we understand what biblical writers meant by the terms they used. To them "faith" or "believed" meant instant infinitely more than merely giving mental assent to an idea. It meant that, but in addition it was used to express the manner by which spiritual truth was perceived and spiritual knowledge gained. There was also an act, one which Connor called "venture," in which one dare to entrust his total being into the control of another, nothing less than the domination of life by Jesus Christ.[2] So, the believer was not one who thought certain things were true for the demons did that. He was one who lived as a man who belonged to Jesus Christ. This response of man results in "salvation." To biblical writers that word did have a negative meaning: deliverance from danger. In the New Testament the emphasis is on that danger which is in sin, and

---

[2] W. T. Conner, *Revelation and God* (Nashville: Broadman Press, 1943), 130.

the deliverance is not merely from punishment, like hell, but from the utter destruction of the total person by evil. But we have erred in making this a full meaning of the word. In both testaments the primary meaning was positive, that is, the fulfillment of one's potential. So, in the New Testament "salvation" means that in Christ man's problems as a sinner are met and overcome by the power of God himself and that his life is filled out to the dimension of God's glory.

Another term which describes this experience is "eternal life." It is unfortunate that we have given it a temporal idea, making it a synonym for "never ending." The biblical words were literally "the life of the ages," a term which did carry a temporal thought, but not of duration (months or years), nor of past or future, but of God's marvelous "now." Its main thought, however, was qualitative, picturing a life in which men experienced the personal infusion of God and all that he, the man, was. Williams translates John 17:3, "Now eternal life means knowing you as the only true God and knowing Jesus your messenger as Christ." The hope of heaven is seen as a natural end of such a life, but without this life there is no biblical promise of heaven to anyone.

Two other closely related terms are of vital importance to understanding this experience. They are "born again" and "son (child) of God." These are commonly interpreted among Baptists to mean that a new spirit nature is injected into man entirely by God's action. Naturally they have occupied an important place in the vocabulary used in the discussion of the believer security. We must remember that they are (1) analogies, descriptive figures, not absolutes, and (2) of Jewish, not American, origin; expressions used by people who thought in practical, not theoretical terms. It is our practice to examine the origin of a person's life to explain its workings and this has a sound psychological basis. They, however, worked on an equally sound basis: they looked at a life as it was lived and derived from what they saw an explanation of its origin; so, to them the person who manifested life of a new order was one who had had a new beginning: he had been born again. It is fallacious mistreatment of New Testament thought to speak of one whose life conforms consistently to the pagan order in which we live as though he has been born again simply because he has stated in some public meeting that he believes in Jesus. In the New Testament the born-again person was the one whose life manifested the power of the polarity of God's grace and man's faith.

The same is true of the term "son (child) of God." To us, the terms of "father" and "son" are primarily biological, meaning 'sire' and 'offspring,' expressing a genetic relationship. Although Jews recognize this usage, they use the terms more to describe a living relationship. The father was one who provided for and guided the development of the child; the son was one who was dependent upon and obedient to the man. This is one force of the biblical analogy; so, by it a son of God was one who lived in dependence upon and obedience to God. In Jewish thought the term son was used also to describe the nature of a person. One who was "a son of" any quality—love, evil, strength, wealth, righteousness—was one whose life was marked by distinct Godlikeness. This is the meaning of the centurion's statement at the foot of the cross, "Truly this was a son of God" (Matthew 27:54). So, both terms which Westerners have used to prove that when one accepts Christ, some mysterious miracle is worked inside him which establishes a permanent, unchangeable relation to God, were used by biblical writers to describe the current life relationship to God. It was not one of only inner or spiritual nature, but one of the total life—the outer as expressive of the inner.

Probably the expression which does as much as any other to muddle the New Testament message for us is the term "gift of God." In Greek, as in English, the term gift is used to represent their present such as is delivered in a package, a thing which is voluntarily presented by one person or group to another. It becomes a complete possession of the receiver, to be used in any way he sees fit. A true gift has no strings on it. This is a picture which most people attach to the word in this usage, giving rise to untold misunderstandings of the gospel message.

By looking farther, we see another common meaning of the word "gift" is capacity, talent, faculty. Then when this thought is coupled with the emphasis of free, unmerited bestowal, we approach the biblical idea. God confers upon man, not a finished, completed product or a fixed result, but the opportunity to participate in the realm of existence which is new to him, "life instead of death." For instance, some fathers face a difficult decision when a son graduates from high school. Should he be given a new car or a college education? The cost could easily be about the same, but in nature the two gifts differ completely. One is a product, brought into existence by other people. It can only be what it is, no matter what the boy may do—with it or without it. The other is opportunity for personal involvement in the struggle called education, and without his involvement, it will have no meaning at all; the gift will not even exist. Through his involvement the son's total life complex will be shaped and directed. The gift itself becomes a power to formulate life as the boy responds in self-discipline. Although it is obviously not a perfect analogy, the college education is far more comparable to the gift of God then is the car. The pole of God's gracious offer to man becomes an effective power only when it is united to the pole of man's voluntary response by participation in the proffered opportunity. Anyone who can read the Greek New Testament will find that this is the kind of person to whom God's wonderful promises to keep and sustain him are made.

In the light of these meanings, we might give another summary of the gospel message. In Christ God has revealed himself by extending to rebellious man the opportunity for a life of restored fellowship with him. When man responds by recognizing Christ as the key to life's realities and commits himself in faith to a living relationship to him, in which Christ is the providing and guiding Lord and the believer is the trusting and obedient son or follower, he experiences the entry of the power of a new life. God becomes a living presence which effects a new approach to both the evil and the potential good of this existence. The man finds life and personal experience. Faith, hope, and love become the essence of the new self which he finds within him. It is one thing to discuss the question of the believer's security with or about this kind of person. It is another thing to discuss it regarding the individuals whose total religious experience has been limited to a type of creedal statement of a faith which affects him no more than the taking of an aspirin, to whom the existence of God is a religious theory, and faith, hope, and love are very empty words. If fruit inspection has any validity, we seem to have far more Baptists of the latter than of the former kind.

There are two areas in which we must try to avoid confusion. Many fine Christians filled with this emphasis opens a way to demand that man merit his salvation by works. Works as used here seems always to refer to something which man does on his own volition to establish his worth. This would take the initiative from God and give it to man. Grace means that God has the initiative always; man can only respond. Just how far will grace pursue a person? Only God knows that; so, it is presumptuous for us to speculate as to when a person is beyond redemption. Who of us could have distinguished clearly between the betrayal of Judas and the denial of Peter if we had been among the disciples on the night of Jesus' arrest. The Hound of Heaven has won many a heart that had strayed far, far away! As surely as we cannot tell how low the ebb of bodily life may sink and that life still be restored, we cannot tell how low it may become in the spirit and yet be restored. So, we can rejoice that the initiative is always with God.

In the same vein men can respond in grace only by faith, never by anything else. This magnifies the personal nature of the relation man with Christ and shows the emptiness of setting up any external standard by which to distinguish between the saved and the unrepentant. The external action which expresses a genuine faith on the part of one person can often be duplicated with ease by another to whom it means nothing. The cramming of life with the most religious of activities may be an effort to find a substitute for the surrender of self to God, which is the essence of faith. In whatever stage it may be—beginning, developing, or consummating—salvation is always by faith on man's part. Too, to biblical people there was so no such distinction as is made using our words "faith" and "faithful." To them the only way one could exercise faith was to be faithful. Hence we need to be careful about how we discuss the self-contradictory idea of the "unfaithful believer" or of the "saved soul and lost life," remembering that as far as we are told, it was on the cross that the dying thief had his first opportunity to respond to Jesus; so, he is no fit example for holding out hope for the individual who professed discipleship, lived a life of utter indifference to Jesus Christ, and "went to meet his reward." It is when man decides to follow God's call that grace is matched with faith and the spark of living power is produced. When one tries to produce the same spark with anything less than obedience, it is like trying to ground an electric wire using a rubber hose; the outward form is there, but the power is missing.

What, then, shall we as Baptist preachers say to these things? What Southern Baptist needs is not an answer to the question, "Is the believer in Christ secure?" They need a solution to the problem of which worry over this question is a symptom, an inadequate living relationship to

God. Our responsibility in this involves at least two things. First, we must dedicate ourselves to the work of securing a clear understanding of the biblical message and expressing it in language which the people of our time understand. Shoddy homework makes for damning preaching. Our greatest shortcoming, the source of our greatest problem, does not lie in our preaching about God and his work in redemption, but rather in failure to clarify man's role. Achieving this must begin by enabling people to come to an awareness of self. Jesus was what he was because he was the truly polarized person. The spirit was as real to him as flesh because he kept his total nature alive, the 100 percent spirit as well as the 100 percent flesh. This is why he was able to stake everything upon the reality of something which no external evidence supported. His invitation, "Follow me," meant, "Let me enable you to practice that which I do." A basic rule of living applies alike to spirit and flesh: that which is used lives and grows; that which is left unused dies. Above all things modern man needs to polarize his being through the conscious life of the spirit in relation to the flesh.

Too, man needs to learn the true meaning of his own freedom. He always wants to live without restraint, but this has brought him nothing but the chains of slavery. Jesus said, "If you continue in my word ... you shall know the truth and that truth will make you free" (John 8:32). The polarity of existence decrees that the only true freedom man can have is under the discipline of God's sovereignty. Only thus can man ever realize the potential of his true self, and this includes Baptists.

Even more must we learn to polarize our faith with God's grace. God offers us life, whole and complete, which is subject to all the basic rules of living; so, only he who will live can have it. He who wears a choir robe and sits in the loft, then refuses to sing, need never fear laryngitis; he has no song to lose. This has been forgotten as we have confused life with attaining status, occupying a position which is static. When Southern Baptists learn anew that there is nothing static about faith in Christ, nothing less than throwing oneself into a headlong venture of obedience to God, just as Jesus did, they will also learn the meaning of "Peace I leave with you. My peace I give to you; not as the world gives, give I to you" (John 14:27). Then the obsession with the theoretical security, of theological proposition, will have vanished because they will have found it alive at the only place where Jesus ever offered it to men—on a cross of their very own.

So, this whole question must never be looked upon as a matter of establishing a theological verity by statements of truth recorded under the Spirit's inspiration, but of recognizing that the scriptures show it to be one of accepting a life which only God can enable to a person to know. One of the great human problems is the perpetual desire to possess that which can be had only by a given process— without going through the process. This produces short-cut seekers. And this is what faith is when it is no more than the middle acceptance of an idea, a substitute for involvement in life itself and fellowship with God. This, however, is like most of the other such efforts to find a shorter, easier way; it is a short-circuit, not a short-cut. This effort continues, however, because men want to be privileged spectators, guests of the team who share the thrills of the game and the jubilation of the team in victory—without putting out the energy and suffering the bruises of participation. That is not the way of New Testament faith. The problem might be called the bargain basement complex, the desire to get as much of the idea of value as can be gotten at the lowest possible price. The great sin of Baptist teaching, however unintended it may have been, has been the development of a system of thinking which makes it mentally and spiritually acceptable for a person to profess to be a believer in Jesus Christ, to sit down with utter impunity and ignore the call of God to follow on in the path of discipleship, then to use the scriptures to prove that absolutely no real harm can befall him for it. In the New Testament the promise of security to the believer is meant to be a pillar of certainty for the concern; we have sought to make it a pillow of ease for the indifferent. One thing must be made clear to Southern Baptists: The New Testament offers no privileged spectator status; no basement type bargains to anyone. There is only one price for all—a cross!

The second thing we can do is to provide a living example of that which we preach. Our job is not merely to call men into a self-forgetting faith in Jesus Christ as the Lord of life; it is more to say as Paul did, "Be imitators of me just as I also am of Christ" (I Corinthians 11:1). In trying to describe this kind of faith Donald G. Miller said:

> John Bunyan, lying in Bedford Jail, fearing lest he should be beheaded for his faithfulness, tells us what faith is in some of the most moving words ever recorded in the literature of the soul. He writes: "I am for going on, and venturing my eternal state with Christ, whether I have comfort here or not ... I will

leap off the ladder even blindfolded into eternity, sink or swim, come heaven, come hell. Lord Jesus, if thou wilt catch me, do; if not, I will venture for thy name." That is faith! And that is the sort of faith out of which Bunyan's faithfulness grew.[3]

Do you think that John Bunyan would have wasted one minute in philosophical argument over the doctrine of the security of the believer? I don't! When believing Jesus comes to mean to us what it meant to him, neither will we. When our study of the scriptures leads us to the practice of that kind of faith, we will better understand the psalmists' confession, "Yea though I walk through the valley of the shadow of death, I will fear no evil; for thou art with me." And we will not wonder why the soon-to-be-executed Paul could say, "I know whom I have believed and am persuaded that he is able to keep my commitment until that day" II Timothy 1:12). If or when it happens, both we and those people who follow us will soar high above the problems which so burden us today. We will make a meaningful beginning if we make these words of Washington Gladden our own prayer.

O master, let me walk with Thee
    In lowly paths of service free;
Tell me thy secret, help me bare
The strain of toil, the fret of care.

Help me the slow of heart to move
By some clear, winning word of love:

---

[3] Donald G. Miller, "On Rejoicing in God," *Interpretation* II (April 1948): 178f.

Teach me the wayward feet to stay,
And guide them in the homeward way.

Teach me Thy patience; still with Thee
In closer, dearer company,
In work that keeps faith sweet and strong,
In trust that triumphs over wrong.

In hope that sends a shining ray
Far down the future's broadening way,
In peace that only thou canst give,
With Thee, O Master, let me live.

Convocation Address
Midwestern Baptist Theological Seminary

By Dr. William B. Coble

January 27, 1984

LIFE IN CHRIST, LEARNING TO THINK
THE WAY GOD THINKS

Introduction

No vehicle can convey the appreciation, gratitude, and affection that I feel for this group of comely gentlemen who are so academically festooned. For more years than many of you have lived they have been gracious, understanding, and uplifting to me in every possible way. I am sure of one thing about them: they know the meaning of life in Christ.

So, in preparing this paper I determined to try to speak directly to you who are students, for whose benefit Southern Baptists established and maintain this seminary. The public statement of purpose says, "Midwestern Seminary seeks primarily to prepare men and women to minister." So, we of the faculty are in the position that Paul described to the Corinthian church. "People should regard us as servants of Christ and stewards of God's revealed secrets. Moreover, it is required of stewards that they be found worthy of trust (I Corinthians 4:1–2).

The thoughts of scores of teachers and writers have helped shape this paper, but for brevity's sake I am citing none of them except the writers of scripture. The teachings have become a part of myself; so, these are my words to you, offered with the anticipation that you will receive them as they are spoken—with a genuine faith, a bright hope, and a lot of love.

The Issue of Life

Life in Christ is the goal of all biblical teaching. The scriptures show the process by which this life became possible, and they go to great lengths to teach us what that life is—and what it is not. We are still living in the backwash of the great wave that generally released the idea of life in Christ from the widespread control of authoritarian churches. Now many are floundering among those who insist that life in Christ comes through any kind of faith that one holds sincerely, especially if that sincere holder can quote scripture.

Values from the Scriptures

The scriptures are for us, the primary source of two great values. One, we may call the bright side; since it opens to us the ways God has unfolded his self-revelation. We can know that the kind of person he is and the way he can embody himself and those who know him because they trust him and obey him. They illustrate the working of one of life's axioms: people develop in the likeness of the God they serve. These realities work together to aid us to understand and to adopt the way God thinks.

The other side of the scriptures' values is the way they show us the nature, working, and results of human kinds of thinking about God. We can call it the dark side of the revelation; since in it we hear God's continued calls for his people to repent—change their ways of thinking and walk in his chosen paths. But why do we have that dark side? It is a major key to our understanding people's continual efforts to claim God's promises of blessing while so modifying God's stated purposes and ways that they will fit comfortably into patterns shaped by their own choices. Those patterns make self-life's center; so, God becomes an adjunct, supposedly available to empower the people to achieve their objectives. The forms in which that reality has taken in the past stand as warnings that we never think ourselves immune to the tendency.

Ancient Ways of Modifying God

The scriptures tell us of four major patterns by which people try to modify God to fit their preferences. The first was a form of nature religion. For centuries the people under covenant to worship only the personal, living God yielded to the attraction of the Baals, deities that offered security, prosperity, and comfort in exchange for people's performing correct religious rituals. But the great tragedy of the Old Testament lay in the people's supposedly rejecting Baalism, only to worship the Lord as though he were

Baal. But beware of a too pious condemnation of those wayward ancients. Listen and carefully watch; then consider how churches, literature, and broadcast media keep telling people that if they will only believe in Jesus, they will be secure, prosperous, and happy. That Baalism has been adapted to fit modern America's sensitivities, but its nature remains the same—self-serving.

The second phase of modifying God's ways developed in reaction to both the first folly and the devastation the Assyrians and Babylonians had wreaked on the people. Jews who returned from exile in Babylon were committed to have no part in idolatry. Their alternative was total commitment to the Lord's covenant teaching (Torah). To retain their identity as the Lord's people, the Jews waged a centuries-long battle with encroaching Semitic, Greek, and Roman pagans. That struggle to be faithful to God tempered the souls of the faithful. It also honed to a sharp edge two powerful forces in Jewish life: a nationalism that burned to consume the Gentiles, and the conviction that observing the Torah validated Israel as the earth's only people of God. The process also tended to give teaching the force of law. Israel hoped that careful keeping of the Torah's rigid rules and practicing its many rituals would bring the fulfillment of God's purposes for the earth— give Israel ruling control. Jesus had to meet that system head on; yet the system has always been a powerful force in shaping the thought and conduct of many professed followers of Jesus. Again, listen and look carefully. How much of professed Christian preaching and teaching calls for God's people to keep rules rigidly and observe prescribed rituals meticulously?

The third major phase of the modification problem combined elements of the first two phases with elements of popular Greek thought. The combined ideas plagued early Christian churches over the Roman Empire, then took form in the numerous branches of the Gnosticism, which many call the first great Christian heresy. That system promised individual salvation to each one who would learn the secret knowledge that God had revealed to his chosen. That knowledge would give the person's spirit (good) release from its prison of the material body (evil). Continued physical life became an amoral wait until death released the redeemed spirit to go directly to God. If you will again look and listen, you will see that Gnostic thinking is also a powerful force in our own churches.

The fourth phase of modification problem is more difficult to designate. We could call it the apostles' creed, or the county-seat-church vision, the "more appropriate opportunity to exercise a completely responsible stewardship of my gifts" complex, or even that distasteful dreg from the dictionary—ambition. Whatever we call it, the issue is active self-promotion under the guise of serving God; and this attitude/practice has always been one of the most formidable obstacles to attaining a genuine pattern of God's kind of thinking. Paul was speaking to this problem when he told the Philippians, "Let this mind be in you, which you have in Christ Jesus, who ... emptied himself and took the form of a slave ... and humbled himself ... even to death on a cross" (Philippians 2:5–8).

These four systems have been derivatives and relatives, and all of them express human kinds of

thinking about God. They present appealingly,
at least, two major fallacies: Mankind has ways
to merit God's blessings; and God gives his favor-
ites power to gain and exercise dominating control over others. This view of the nature and the
working of divine power is at the heart of human
evil.

Jesus /Christ, The Gospels, and Interpretations

God's self-revelation in Jesus Christ is the
foundation of our understanding of the way God
thinking differs from any form of human thinking. Christians differ over the place to begin the
study of that revelation. Many start with Paul's
theology. I strongly believe that we must start
with the Gospels.

For at least seventeen centuries New Testament students have debated the differences
between John and the Synoptic Gospels (Matthew, Mark, and Luke). A majority has always
assumed or concluded that the differences are
evidence that the writers held differing views
of Jesus, his nature, life, purpose, and methods.
Prior to World War II, most New Testament
scholars held that the Synoptic writers tended
to provide essential historical accounts of Jesus'
ministry, while John gave a theological interpretation. Many still hold this view. But the theory
leaves at least two major problems. First, in the
Synoptics the weeks that ended with the crucifixion was Jesus' only visit to Jerusalem during his
ministry. If that was the case, we cannot account
for the events that visit produced. So, can we
truly view those accounts as objective history?
Also, most interpretations of the Synoptics long

have been based on the geographical areas of Jesus ministries—Galilee, Gentile areas around Galilee, Perea, Judea, and Jerusalem. The result has been most often a collection of devotional or independently theological interpretations of a series of seemingly unrelated events and teachings. These handlings make any clear picture of Jesus' purpose almost impossible. But the greatest lack is a consistent explanation of why his life had to end on the cross. Why anybody would have bothered to crucify the Jesus whom most of those interpretations picture remains one of history's insoluble riddles.

Since World War II, many interpreters using redaction critical studies have each gospel as a theological interpretation of Jesus and his ministry. For many, the approach has magnified the difference between John and the Synoptics. Nobody can seriously ignore the ways John's Gospel does differ from the three. But I'm convinced that great loss has resulted from overlooking major bonds of unity within the four. To perceive the common foci, one must study each Gospel as a literary unit until the developments that each one presents becomes clear. Then the relationships between the books themselves will become more apparent. Any effort to establish unity by focusing on literary or historical relationships between isolated texts is foredoomed.

The Nature of Jesus Christ, the Basis of the Gospel's Unity

My thesis is that the foundation of the Gospel's unity is their presentation of Jesus as the Lord's Suffering Servant Messiah of Israel. That presentation pictures God's supreme self-revelation as self-giving devotion to the welfare of (agape for) his rebellious creation. Here we can look only at the Gospels' central structure.

The Beginnings: Jesus' Knowledge of his Purpose

<u>The Synoptic Gospels.</u> --The Synoptics have almost identical skeletons, although they are filled out quite differently. Their accounts of Jesus begin with John the Baptist, whose ministry involved two major factors. His baptism of repentance was nothing less than a demand that people begin obeying God's revealed will. John also identified Jesus as the one who would baptize people with the Holy Spirit. Remembering this introductory statement is vital to grasping these Gospel's central message.

The Synoptic story of Jesus hinges on three pivotal points: Jesus' baptism and temptation in the wilderness; the confession and the teachings at Caesarea Philippi; and the crucifixion and resurrection.

The baptism and temptation experiences introduced the Servant Messiah. Jesus accepting John's baptism means that Jesus also committed himself to obey God's revealed will. Many have trouble with this truth. Emphasis on the deity of Christ has blinded them to a self-evident fact: the gospels present the life and work of the person whom the people of the time saw as a human being like themselves.

Having committed himself to obey God, Jesus' experienced three realities. He saw the heavens opened (God was present), and he saw the Holy Spirit come down (from the heavens) into him. Thus, he received God's wisdom and power to act. Then Jesus heard. "You are my beloved son" refers to Psalms 2:7, which identified God's designated king over Israel (the Messiah or the Christ). "With whom I am well pleased" refers to Isaiah 42:1, the beginning of Isaiah's famous servant songs, which came to their climax in the descriptions of the servant sufferings, in Isaiah 52:13–53:12. Thus God's revealed will for Jesus (his assignment) presented a great paradox for every Jew. Jesus must become Israel's ruler as the Lord's Servant, who suffers at the hands of evil men. Jews had never made that connection; since, like every paradox, the two terms seem self-contradictory. How could a lowly servant be the deliverer of any oppressed people?

The indwelling Holy Spirit led Jesus into a period of having his commitment to his assignment tested by his arch enemy, the accuser, the spirit of total evil. Matthew and Luke described what Mark only implies. Satan did not test Jesus at the point of his being the Messiah but at the point of his servanthood. He appealed to Jesus to show God's self-giving love by providing Israel a kind of Messiah they wanted, who would make God's power available to fulfill their personal ambitions and national hopes. That approach would guarantee Jesus' own acceptance and immediate success. Satan tried to get Jesus to think of God's purpose as man thinks, that God supremely reveals himself and his people by giving them the power to exercise domination of others, so-called righteous authority.

Thus, the Synoptics provided a veiled expression of the way Jesus learned and accepted the nature of his ministry and his destiny. From the beginning he knew what others could not grasp. He also knew the evil source of all the opposition to that form of ministry that he kept facing; for those same temptations kept appealing to him at every turn. Some of the last words he heard were, "Come down now from the cross, that we may see and believe" (Mark 15:32).

John's Gospel.—John's gospel does not tell of Jesus' baptism and wilderness temptation, but it gives a similarly valued presentation of the same truths. The testimony of the Baptist identified Jesus as the Messiah and affirmed the Holy Spirit's coming to indwell him: "And John bore witness, 'I saw the Spirit descend as a dove from heaven, and it remained on him. I myself did not know him; but he who sent me to baptize with water said to me, "He on whom you see the Spirit descend and remain, this is he who baptizes with the Holy Spirit." And I have seen and borne witness that this is the son of God'" (John 1:32–34).

The two central events of chapter 2 also present a veiled statement that Jesus' role was to be the Lord's servant, manifesting himself through crucifixion and resurrection. The first of Jesus' signs, turning water into wine at the wedding of Cana of Galilee, taught many vital lessons. Most of them had immediate application. But the importance of the event in the central message of the book hinged on the enigmatic exchange between Jesus and his mother (John 2:3–4).

The exchange introduces the fact that John attributes to Jesus' family a major part of the role that the Synoptics attribute to Satan. The first phase of this function was Jesus' mother's words, "They have no wine." As every effective temptation must be, these words seem totally innocent, treating an inconvenience for celebration. But consider three matters: (1) She knew Jesus had no money to buy wine; so, if he did anything about the dearth, he would have to produce it himself. (2) She knew that he had begun the ministry for which he was born. What more appropriate opportunity could he ask for openly declaring himself as the solver of Israel's problems? (3) Jesus' answer shows that he knew she was making a bold suggestion concerning the way he should conduct his ministry. This setting gave her words the same implications as the words of the wilderness, "Command these stones to become bread" (Matthew 4:3). 'You must be the supplier of Israel's great needs. Begin now!'

So, he asked an idiomatic question, "Lady, what (is common) between you and me?" He told her that she was not thinking the way he was thinking. "My hour has not yet come" had a double meaning, as so many of John's expressions carry. The open meaning was a time to manifest myself has been set, and implied method of his self-manifestation. This meaning becomes clear only by tracing the use of the terms "hour" and "time" (appropriate occasion) through the whole book.

Jesus' brothers took up the family's tempter role, speaking as unbelievers (John 7:3–4). They meant, "If these things you are doing are supposed to show people anything, go where the important people are, Judea (where the leading authorities were centered). They continued their mother's line: 'Showing people is the only way to accomplish what you want; so, the feast of tabernacles would be a most appropriate setting.' But Jesus said, "My time has not yet come, but your time is always here. The world cannot hate you, but it hates me because I testify to it that its works are evil. Go to the feast yourselves; I am not going up to the feast for my time has not fully come." (John 7:5–8). Jesus later did go to Jerusalem and engaged leaders in a bitter argument. "So, they sought to arrest him; but no one laid hands on him, because his hour had not yet come" (John 7:30). The confrontation continued to John 8:20: "No one arrested him because his hour had not yet come." After his acclaimed entry into Jerusalem and some Greeks wanted to talk with him, Jesus said "The hour has come for the Son of man to be glorified" (John 12:23); then he asked, "What shall I say, Father, save me from this hour? No, for this purpose I have come to this hour. Father, glorify thy name" (John 12:27–28a). (In that monologue John described the inner struggle that the Synoptics present in the Gethsemane story, with the same conclusion.) The story of Jesus' private ministry has this introduction, "When Jesus knew that his hour had come to depart out of this world to the Father" (John 13:1). Jesus also began his priestly prayer in John 17:1 by saying, "Father, the hour has come; glorify thy Son that the Son may glorify thee." These uses show that John intended for the words used at Cana to provide a veiled statement of Jesus' coming death, which statement any reader could fully appreciate only at the end of the book.

The second event in John 2 is the cleansing of the temple. After the furor settled, the Jews said to him, "What sign do you show for doing this?" (John 21:8). Jesus faced a demand that was quite comparable to the wilderness suggestion that he leap off the pinnacle of the temple. The authorities wanted a demonstration that would prove Jesus' divine authority, something that no normal person could do, and no normal person could watch without recognizing that God's power was at work. Jesus gave them no act but a statement, the promise of an act that no normal person could see or appreciate without being under the control of God's spirit. "Destroy this sanctuary, and in three days I will raise it up…." but he spoke of the sanctuary of his body. When, therefore, he was raised from the dead, the disciples remembered that he had said this, and they believed the scripture and the statement that Jesus had made" (John 2:18–22). Thus, through these veiled accounts John also shows that from the beginning of his work Jesus knew that the nature of his ministry and of his destiny was that of the Suffering Servant, although nobody else knew.

Jesus' Early Ministry

In the early accounts of Jesus' ministry, the synoptics are closely parallel. But they differ completely from John in details, such as geographical setting, events, and supporting characters. Yet all the Gospels have four major areas of common emphasis. First, Jesus was acting out his row. Yet in the Synoptics he never told anyone that he was either the Messiah or the Servant. Although in John Jesus told the Samaritan woman plainly, "I am he" (the Messiah, John 4:26), he said nothing specific about servanthood. Jesus' deeds and teachings were the media through which people had to understand and evaluate him.

Second, Jesus' followers were slow and hesitant to perceive who and what he was or to give him their genuine, complete trust. (Compare Mark 4:35–41 and pars.; Mark 8:14–21, Matthew 16:5–12 with John 2:23–25; John 6:25–66; John 8:30–59).

Third, Jesus initiated intense, repeated confrontations with the Jewish leadership over the way their strict adherence to rules and rituals interpreted God's character and his purpose for his people. Thus, Jesus showed the great difference between servanthood and servitude. Being the Lord's servant was Jesus' trusting obedient embodiment of God's grace and agape for the sinful and the needy. Servitude is external humiliation and loss of one's personhood by others' use of oppressive, dominating power. Being God's Servant was unrelated to being servile.

Fourth, because of the confrontations that this seemingly bull-headed rebel provoked, Jewish leaders saw him as a threat to Israel's loyalty to the Torah, with the devastating effect that such deviation would have on the people's relationship with God; so, the leaders began examining the need to take serious action. They soon reached the conclusion that he had to die (Mark 3:6 and pars.; John 11:53).

Jesus' Telling the Disciples Who He Was

<u>At Caesarea Philippi</u>. —The pivotal point in the Synoptic Gospels is the experience at Caesarea Philippi (Mark 8:27–9:1, Matthew 16:13–28; Luke 9:18–27). Jesus made sure that the disciples were convinced that he was the Messiah. Then he shocked them with a stern prohibition:

"Don't you dare tell anyone!" And he begins telling them what his being the Messiah meant—suffering, rejection by Israel's leaders, death, and resurrection. This new idea became his continual theme. The disciples could not fail to understand what he meant: nor could they change the subject. Yet they could make no peace with the shift. Finally, the twelve let Peter speak for them. He forcibly told Jesus that such could not be true since that is not the Messiah's function or destiny. You must be Israel's deliverer from their oppressors. Jesus saw the familiar face and heard the clear words from a well-known voice. But he knew who the true enemy was, the same voice he had heard in the wilderness. The tempter must be treated as the tempter: "Out of my site, you devil! Your whole thought system is man-made; it has no relationship to God's truth" (Mark 8:33; Matthew 16:23). (Luke did not relate Jesus' confrontation with Peter (Luke 9:18–27); since Luke had already introduced others' perception of the Servant role (Luke 2:22–38). Luke also had told how Jesus had given a previous public statement on this matter at Nazareth, where the violent rejection had already occurred (Luke 4:16–30).

Then Jesus began teaching the realities of discipleship, how to begin thinking as God thinks (Mark 8:34–9:1 and pars). One must adopt the servant way of obedience to God. Giving up man's kind of thinking can be nothing less than dying to self-centered life. Only then can one truly follow (imitate) Jesus. Possibly the most overlooked words of this paragraph are the eschatological warning: "For whoever is ashamed of me and my words, of him will the Son of man be ashamed when he comes in the glory of his

Father with the holy angels" (Mark 8:38). The meaning is simple: we have no way to adjust or adapt the true Messiah's message or methods. We can accept only the Servant Messiah in full, or we reject him. Only recently have I been gripped with the pathos with which Jesus must have said, "To the road that leads to life, the gate is narrow, and the way the sorely afflicted; and so few find it" (Matthew 7:14).

The disciples had a rough week before Jesus took Peter, James, and John to a mountain where they saw Jesus' true glory shine through, assuring them that God was within him. Then from the cloud that came over them, indicating God's presence (see Exodus 40:34–38), the voice that Jesus had heard at his baptism told the disciples, "This is my beloved son (the Messiah): you keep listening to him" (Mark 9:7). The message meant, 'Difficult as it is to accept, he is telling you the truth.'

After that experience the Synoptics tell of a series of events in which Jesus kept teaching the disciples how to learn to think as God thinks. These events bring their story to Jesus' entry into Jerusalem under the acclaim of the crowds.

<u>Jesus' Declaration to the Multitudes</u>.—All four Gospels include the event that has been so mistakenly called "The Triumphal Entry" because it has been treated most often as an isolated event. And for centuries interpreters focused on the crowd's words to Jesus rather than on Jesus' message to them. But each Gospel shows that this act of riding a donkey colt was Jesus' climatic effort to see him as the Servant King, as pictured in Zechariah 9:9–10. Yet they hailed him as the Davidic King for which they yearned, pleading that he bring them deliverance from the Romans

as David had delivered Israel from the Philistines. No matter how Jesus tried to show the public that he was the Servant, they insisted that he must fill the role that the tempter tried to entice him to accept in the wilderness, the great wonder-working deliverer. They were saying, 'We want you to change the conditions around us; since we intend to remain what we are. This event introduced the last week of Jesus' life, leading to his death and resurrection.

<u>Washing the Disciples' Feet.</u>—Jesus' washing the disciples' feet is the event that serves in John's Gospel the function that the Synoptics' Caesarea Philippi experience served. Throughout most of history this fact seems to have been overlooked. The reason probably lies in the history of interpretation. For centuries people assumed that the Gospels were detailed, literal history. They could see no reason to suppose that Jesus introduced a new concept to his followers during this last week of his life; since the synoptics clearly said that he had been teaching the same truth for months before he came to Jerusalem. The early literary critics supposedly demonstrated that Mark presented the true historical sequence of Jesus' ministry (The Markan Hypothesis); so, they undergirded the ancient view. In that light interpreters almost had to conclude that here Jesus was giving the group a supplementary lesson on humility or some such subject.

This situation serves to underscore the differences between the structure of John's account and the structure of Synoptics' accounts. So, we must not base our understanding of John's message on the schedule of events presented in the Synoptics. But once a perception or interpretation of a text becomes thoroughly established, any major change occurs very slowly.

John's account clearly leaves room for us to assume that the disciples had come to this meal 'higher than most kites' because of the reception that Jesus had received on entering the city. John had said in chapter 12:16 that, as in the temple cleansing of chapter 2, the disciples did not at that time understand the meaning of the message Jesus delivered by his entry into the city. All they could see was their coming political and military glory. Even the Pharisees had said to each other in despair, "You can see that you can do nothing; look, the world has gone after him" (John 12:19).

The assembly around the table reflected the same attitude that the disciples exhibited in Mark's story of Peter's confession. The evidence of the disciples' obsession with their own self-importance was their ignoring the washbasin. Custom dictated that each one washes his own feet on entering the room. But people of the standing that they expected to achieve assumed that someone else would wash their feet on such a gala occasion—a kind of pre-coronation banquet. John gave the reason Jesus washed their feet: "Knowing that the Father had given all things into his hands, and that he had come from God and was going to God" (verse 3). Nobody and no act could add anything to Jesus' status or take anything from it. So, he was free. The disciples were prisoners of their own obsessive ambitions. By disrobing and girding himself with a towel, Jesus delivered a symbolic lesson, as many of the prophets had done. His standing before them in that way said, 'Look, I am the slave.' Then he began acting the part of the lowliest (Gentile) slave (Jewish slaves usually did not have to wash their owner's feet).

Peter objected—first politely, then stubbornly: "You will never wash my feet" (verse 8). Jesus' reply had the same meaning as Mark 8:38: 'If you are ashamed of me as I am, there is nothing between us; I cannot become something other than myself to suit your preferences' (verse 8b). Then Peter melted.

Just as Caesarea Philippi exchange with the disciples was the background for a long section of instruction on learning to think as God thinks (Mark 8:34—10:52), Jesus' washing the disciples' feet was the background for a long section of instruction on the kind of faith that produces eternal life (John 13:12—16:33; see John 20:30–31). That life grows within the habit of obeying God by the Spirit's guidance and power.

The Servant's Triumph

The apex of all the Gospels is the story of the crucifixion and resurrection. Differing details appear in all four accounts, but no serious doubt can exist that they are telling the same central story. We must understand that in all of them the cross itself was the glory of both God and Christ. It was not a necessary, temporary step along the way to a final exercise of dominating power over all the world. The power that brings human life to its full meaning works through total self-giving as life's ultimate glory. Thus, anyone who would share God's life and thinking must realize that the only place he can choose to stop following Jesus is above the ground atop Calvary.

Francis of Assisi's famous prayer has moved all of us many times. It consists of two parts. First is this series of soul-searching petitions:

> Lord, make me an instrument of your peace;
> where there is hatred, let me sow love; where there is injury, pardon;
> where there is doubt, faith; where there is despair, hope;
> where there is darkness, light; where there is sadness, joy.
> O Diving Master, grant that I may not so much seek to be consoled as to console;
> to be understood as to understand; to be loved as to love;

Then comes a three-point rationale:

For it is in giving that we receive; it is in pardoning that we are pardoned;

To this point these beautiful expressions draw the approving response of perceptive people from most of the religious faiths of the world. Even interested, warm-hearted, generous humanist philosophers can join freely in most of the expressions. So where do we find any uniquely Christian perspective? Only in the last line:

<u>And it is in dying that we are born to eternal life. Amen.</u>

As our Master said from the lake front of Galilee, the byways of Judea, and the shoreline of Patmos: "You who have ears to hear, listen!"

Bibliography

The following are books that were written by William B. Coble:

Messages from First Century Christians. Nashville: Convention Press, 1971.

Study Guide to Matthew. Nashville: Sunday School Board of the Southern Baptist Convention, 1975.

The Person and Work of Christ: A Study in the Gospel According To Mark. Sunday School Board of the Southern Baptist Convention, 1969.

Christ, The Lord of All; A Study in Colossians. Sunday School Board, Southern Baptist Convention, 1969.

"Old Testament Doctrine of Grace as Seen in Hebrew Terminology." PhD diss., Southwestern Baptist Theological Seminary, 1956.

Here is a list of books where the author William B. Coble was a contributor:

Children and Conversion, edited by Clifford Ingle. Nashville Broadman Press, 1970.

Wycliffe Bible Encyclopedia, 2 vols., edited By Charles F. Pfeiffer et al. Chicago Moody Press, 1975.

The Teacher's Bible Commentary. "Chapter on Revelation" edited by H. Franklin Paschall and Hershel H. Hobbs. Nashville, Tennessee: Broadman Press, 1972.

"Sunday School Lessons." *Word and Way* (Journal of Missouri Baptist Convention) (May 1972 to the 1980s).

About the Author

Douglas W. Crabb attended Oklahoma Baptist University where he earned his bachelor of arts degree. He then went to Midwestern Baptist Theological Seminary in Kansas City, Missouri, where he earned his master of divinity degree and his doctor of ministry degree. The focus of his doctorate degree was on theological reflection in the life of the local church. Doug and his wife, Sheila, were married in 1972. They have two adult children and four grandchildren. In 2003, Doug was diagnosed with a malignant brain tumor. He underwent two brain surgeries, chemotherapy, and radiation treatments. He has now been cancer-free for over twenty years.